MANAGING BUSINESS CRISES

MANAGING BUSINESS CRISES

From Anticipation to Implementation

John Burnett

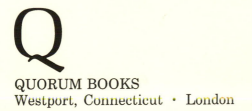

QUORUM BOOKS
Westport, Connecticut · London

Library of Congress Cataloging-in-Publication Data

Burnett, John.
   Managing business crises : from anticipation to implementation / John Burnett.
      p.   cm.
   Includes bibliographical references.
   ISBN 1–56720–404–X (alk. paper)
   1. Industrial management. 2. Crisis management. I. Title.
HD31.B78   2002
658.4′056—dc21   2002024803

British Library Cataloguing in Publication Data is available.

Library of Congress Catalog Card Number: 2002024803
ISBN: 1–56720–404–X

First published in 2002

Quorum Books, 88 Post Road West, Westport, CT 06881
An imprint of Greenwood Publishing Group, Inc.
www.quorumbooks.com

Printed in the United States of America

∞™

The paper used in this book complies with the
Permanent Paper Standard issued by the National
Information Standards Organization (Z39.48–1984).

10 9 8 7 6 5 4 3 2 1

Contents

Figures and Tables

FIGURES

TABLES

Introduction:
Were You Prepared?

The Chinese use two brush strokes to write the word "crisis." One brush stroke stands for danger; the other for opportunity. In a crisis, be aware of the danger—but recognize the opportunity.

Richard M. Nixon

SEPTEMBER 11, 2001

Were you prepared for the events of that day, and the subsequent changes in our homes, schools, and businesses?[1] Much has been said about the fact that America "will never be the same again." But, in what ways? Whether we will relearn to live without fear, regain our economic stability, or rekindle the spirit of opportunity for which the United States of America is so well known, is not in doubt. But how do we move from initial danger to eventual opportunity?

Some would say that "only time will tell," "time heals all wounds," or "give it time," but this text suggests that each of us can have more of an effect on our corporate destinies. Organizations must change and adapt to survive—an old adage. The hypothesis that led to the writing of this book reflects the duality so well penned by Richard Nixon—within every crisis lies the seeds of success, as well as the roots of failure. Opportunity comes with danger. The challenge is to work past the horror and loss, and find a positive outcome. The only way to hope to make it past incidents, accidents, conflicts, or crises is to acknowledge the possibility of their happening, and have a plan for how to prevent and/or respond.

Whether your company was headquartered in one of the World Trade Center towers and lost two-thirds of its staff, all records, computers, and other assets; or the Idaho-based firm for which you work makes plastic trays for airline meals; or you are a ski instructor, cosmetologist, or marketing executive, you will undoubtedly feel the aftershocks of the devastating terrorist attacks (see Figure I.1). That is, if you haven't already. This book seeks to outline ways in which you and your firm can take a proactive approach to crisis management. The concepts of proximity to the danger–crisis, rational versus irrational initial responses, surviving your challenging environment, and the development of a tailored crisis management plan is detailed in the twelve chapters that follow.

This book seeks to give you, the reader, the tools to implement sound plans to manage crisis. Not only does it lay out a case for research, retrospection, goal setting, stakeholder relations, and communication, it pulls together a message: The successful management of crisis starts well in advance of the event, involves every person in the organization, and is not dependent upon individual responses. Right now, in November 2001, while the wounds sustained from the events of September 11 are still raw, perhaps it will be easier to get the company for which you work to pull together and get serious about a crisis plan.

How does this book on crisis management differ from the many others on the same subject? Primarily the difference lies in the breadth taken toward the subject of crisis. In all other crisis management books crisis is equated with catastrophe. These books assume that the only crisis worth managing are those disasters that take lives, cause injuries, or produce major property damage. Thus, these books are most relevant to companies that have a high propensity for disasters. In this book we offer all businesses a paradigm to employ in managing crisis, from minor to major. It is a unique perspective, but one that is needed in this dynamic global business environment.

NOTE

1. The main text of this book was finished and in the editing stage on September 11, 2001. Therefore, the examples that were interwoven with the text were left in place, and the Introduction and Epilogue were added.

Figure I.1
The Outward Spiral of Negative Effects of the Day

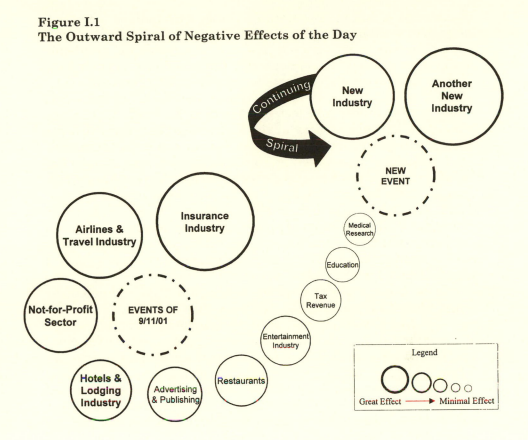

We feel that this does a greater service to the topic: It allows the reader to truly use this text to dissect their own situation. Rather than benchmark all best practices in managing crisis against the worst case in U.S. history, we feel it is important to illustrate that the crisis continuum is a crucial instrument for management. The severity of a disruption does not qualify or disqualify the effect it has on your particular organization. Using the tools outlined in this book, you will be the judge of how best to plan for and manage crisis.

1

Crisis Management in a Nutshell

Next week there can't be any crisis. My schedule is already full.
Henry Kissinger, while Secretary of State

Seven days. That's all the time it took for the 114-year-old Atlanta-based beverage behemoth Coca-Cola Company to go from a much admired and trusted market leader in Europe to a company scrambling to give away products in order to pick up the shreds of consumer confidence.

Seven days was the lag time between the first press reports of children and adults becoming ill after drinking Coca-Cola products in Belgium and Northern France, and a full-scale response from the company acknowledging consumers' concerns—including an apology from former Coke CEO M. Douglas Ivester.

The bruising that Coke's image took after that week holds lessons for all marketers charged with maintaining brand equity. Experts on the company, as well as in the practice of crisis management, say Coke misread consumers' levels of concern when the first reports surfaced. While Coke focused on denying that its product was responsible for the illnesses, the press filled the information vacuum with speculation and accusations from other sources.

Ultimately, the company set up a consumer hotline and offered to pay all medical bills, but no matter: Before Coke had the chance to selectively recall products that may have been part of the afflicted shipments, governments throughout Northern Europe were banning and recalling Coke soft drinks or, in some countries, all Coke products. The battle lines had been drawn.

The problems faced by Coke were enormous, and no one knows what the ultimate consequences will be on sales, brand equity, and goodwill. We do know Coke reported losses of $45 million during the fourth quarter of 1999 and laid off 6,000 employees in 2000. With the need for global media to constantly find stories to spike consumer interest, the odds are that Coke will be reliving the crisis for many years.

In fact, this need for crisis recognition and management has been around for a long time. Throughout history, there has been no shortage of business crises. In 1637, speculation in Dutch tulip bulbs peaked at today's equivalent of more than $1,000 per bulb and the market collapsed under its own weight, presenting financially wrenching crises for speculators and their backers. In 1861, the infant Pony Express met its sudden demise when Western Union inaugurated the first transcontinental telegraph. In 1906, the San Francisco earthquake devastated the city and its banking community—except for A. P. Giannini, whose small Bank of America continued making loans during the crisis and went on to become one of the world's largest banks. In the past few years, a trusted manufacturer of baby food admitted that its apple juice was actually flavored sugar water; syringes inexplicably turned up in the cans of another firm's popular cola brand; and a major oil company's obsolete drilling rig became a rallying point for a radical environmental group.

Almost every crisis contains within itself the seeds of success as well as the roots of failure. Finding, cultivating, and harvesting that potential success is the essence of crisis management. And the essence of crisis mismanagement is the propensity to take a bad situation and make it worse. Assuming that the only crises that need management are those that are considered catastrophes also leads to mismanagement. All crises must be managed; both large and small.

Since the famous Tylenol incident in 1982, when a terrorist poisoned Johnson & Johnson pain relief capsules with cyanide, crisis management has become a booming industry. Companies took note of the public support that occurred when that crisis was dealt with well. They also took to heart the negative reverberations of mishandling a tragedy in the cases of the Union Carbide Bhopal disaster and the Exxon Valdez spill.

Amazingly, however, many companies still fail to put plans in place in anticipation of a catastrophe. As dismaying as it may sound, from 50 to 70 percent of the largest profit-making organizations in the world have not made any disaster plans. The percentage is much higher for small businesses and nonprofit organizations, primarily because they are less likely to have personnel to handle this function. When timing and initial response matter as much, this could be fatal for a company.

Several books and many articles have been written concerning the identification, management, and prevention of business crises. Espousing a proactive rather than a reactive model, they all begin with a basic definition of crisis. What is an organizational crisis? How are crises distinguished from more routine situations? Pauchant and Mitroff provide one definition of crisis. Employing a two-by-two matrix, the authors propose a continuum, beginning with an incident, continuing with an accident, followed by conflict, and ending with a crisis, the most serious form of disruption (see Figure 1.1).

In this context, a crisis is "a disruption that physically affects a system as a whole and threaten its basic assumptions, its subjective sense of self, its essential core." If we accept this notion of crisis, then the majority of what we know about crisis and its management is brought to question. That is, if we place crisis-producing disruptions on a continuum based on level of severity; a mild disruption may not comply with the prescribed definition. And, therefore, the same response to different disruptions is not appropriate. Moreover, other criteria besides severity should be considered in light of the complexity of crisis management.

THE DESIRED PERSPECTIVE

One thing is for certain, crisis management, regardless of parameters, requires that strategic action be taken both to avoid or mitigate undesirable developments, and to bring about a desirable resolution of the problems noted. Moreover, crisis management must be an inherent element of the corporate culture, as well as a continu-

Figure 1.1
Crisis Continuum

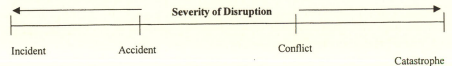

Severity of Disruption

Incident   Accident   Conflict

Catastrophe

ous management effort. Unfortunately, crisis management represents a strategic issue that looms as one most difficult to resolve because of the additional elements of poor understanding of the concept, along with time pressure, limited control, and high uncertainty.

This book offers a strategic model that attempts to deal with the limitations found in the existing crisis management literature and extends to a totally integrated approach to crisis management. This model is depicted in Figure 1.2 and serves as the framework for our discussion. Before we begin the discussion it is useful to review some of the key literature on crisis management.

WHAT WE KNOW ABOUT CRISIS MANAGEMENT

Research investigating crisis in business settings has borrowed heavily from a variety of disciplines and, for the most part, the results have been primarily observational. Three general approaches to investigating organizational crisis are evident from a review of the crisis management literature. These research streams are the following: case analysis of organizational crisis, crises prescriptions, and descriptive models of the crisis management process.

Case Analysis

Case studies examine how different organizations deal with crisis. The findings from the research highlighted in these studies can be summarized as follows:

1. *The likelihood of a crisis occurring and the severity of the crisis varies by industry, by company, and by function.* For example, one expert posits that there are nine types of business crisis: (1) public perception, (2) business relations, (3) sudden market shifts, (4) product failure, (5) top management succession, (6) hostile takeovers, (7) regulations and deregulations, (8) adverse international events, and (9) cash crisis. Some suggest that there are high crisis-prone and low crisis-prone businesses.

2. *The solution to a crisis has both short-term and long-term ramifications.* Moreover, companies must be cognizant of both if they are going to provide a permanent solution to a crisis. Companies such as Union Carbide, Dayco, and The Continental Illinois Bank appear to have dealt with the situation at hand with little forethought about the future. In contrast, the rash of hostile takeovers during the 1980s appear to have produced the opposite result. Safeway Stores, Continental Airlines, and others were so preoccupied with potential takeovers that they often created immediate crises (such as store shutdowns, layoffs) just as detrimental.

Figure 1.2
The Crises Planning Process

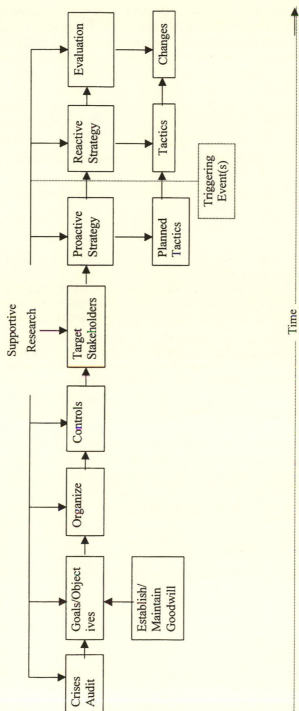

3. *Crisis may produce gains as well as losses.* Crisis produces the following possible gains: (1) heroes are born, (2) changes are accelerated, (3) latent problems are faced, (4) people can be changed, (5) new strategies evolve, (6) early warning systems develop, and (7) new competitive edges appear. Perhaps the most widely publicized businessperson of the 1980s was Lee Iacocca, a man emerging from the dust of a hopeless situation—Chrysler Motors. Conversely, Ramée suggests that a crisis can produce any one or more of the following losses: (1) severe impact on corporate profits, perhaps leading to the demise of the business; (2) unwanted public and government scrutiny; (3) damage to corporate integrity and name; (4) unproductive diversion of employees, time, and capital; and (5) negative employee morale.

4. *There is no systematic or widely accepted strategy for managing crisis.* For example, experts concur that there is only a loose set of guidelines, often including steps for limiting negative consequences to industry-specific crisis.

5. *There are common difficulties associated with the management of crisis.* Examples of such difficulties include uncertainty, poor data-handling methods, too little data, too much data, inadequate communications, differing value systems, changing management objectives, political harassment, little planning, and insufficient time in which to learn.

6. *Organizations are not yet able to calculate the utility functions associated with crisis.* Stated simply, what is the relative trade-off between the costs and benefits of resolving a crisis versus leaving it unresolved. Despite the salience of this issue, it has been given little attention.

In sum, observations of organizational crisis point to the multifaceted nature of this phenomenon. Developing principles that apply to all crises are unlikely, as are general solutions. Moreover, the results reported here refer to a variety of crisis types, but do not delineate the level of severity. Nevertheless, there is a body of literature that proposes prescriptions that, in the opinions of those authors, apply to most types of crises.

Crises Prescriptions

In the second approach to understanding crisis management, the emphasis is primarily on delineating prescriptions for crisis identification and resolution. These prescriptive studies have both general and industry-specific applicability. For example, there is consensus that four major questions should be asked in a crisis situation:

1. Is there really a crisis?
2. If there is a crisis, do I have to act?

3. If I decide to act, when do I make my move?
4. If I act, who should be involved?

McGrath and Pendersen address the crucial problem of one type of crisis—product recall. They present substantial evidence that (1) higher safety expectations and resulting legislation will increase product recall frequency, and (2) the costs and risks associated with product recalls will also increase. Given these trends, they recommend a twelve-step response process that can be reduced to five major considerations: (1) determine the nature of the recall, (2) assemble the recall item, (3) notify all relevant parties, (4) implement the recall, and (5) assess the effectiveness of the recall.

One of the most serious product recalls of the last decade was initiated by Ford Motors and Bridgestone–Firestone tires. On August 9, 2000, Ford's largest tire supplier, Bridgestone–Firestone Inc., said it was recalling 6.5 million tires amid reports linking faulty tires to as many as forty-six deaths in the United States. With at least 1 million Explorers equipped with the faulty 15-inch tires remaining on the highways, estimates of the final costs could exceed $1 billion.

Unfortunately, Ford and Firestone had known about the tire flaws for at least a year, but it wasn't until the National Highway Transportation Safety Administration launched a preliminary investigation that Firestone moved to issue a voluntary recall. It's also unfortunate that the resulting congressional hearing on the Firestone tire recall could have been held twenty-two years ago. In May and July of 1978, executives from Firestone Tire and Rubber Company of Akron, Ohio, sat in front of a House subcommittee for four days, defending a first-generation radial tire called the Firestone 500. Then, as now, the top officers of the company did not admit to a defect in their product, though there were hundreds of complaints about the tire disintegrating on the rim, and forty-one deaths were reported. Appearing before Rep. John Moss, D-California, they blamed the tires problems on bad maintenance and underinflation. Then, as now, members of Congress expressed disbelief and wonderment that the company didn't order a recall sooner. And then, as now, there was testimony about rollovers, improper tire pressure, and examples of how federal tire-testing laws led to missed opportunities to head off the problem. One would have thought Firestone would have learned its lesson.

There will be no Tylenol Award for the Firestone official who, when the news first broke, said, "These things aren't indestructible. They are made out of rubber. Every passenger car sold in the United States is sold with a spare tire, and they're sold with a spare tire for a reason." All the standard PR operating procedures smelled like denial, an odor that will linger even if subsequent investigations show that Firestone's original recall plan was adequate and responsible.

Unfortunately, prescriptive lists such as those just cited offer little new information for managing crisis. Closer scrutiny suggests that these studies are simple extensions of the basic management process and do no necessarily lead to comprehensive strategies. Fortunately, there are a number of strategic models that attempt to address this need.

Crisis Management Models

Descriptive models comprise a third major approach to the study of crisis management. These frameworks, which begin with variable identification and relationship specification, and continue with processes necessary for strategy determination, offer much greater potential than either case analysis or prescriptive studies for furthering our understanding of, and ability to manage, organizational crisis.

There seems to be a general agreement (and some empirical support) that the crisis management process contains five basic components: (1) a set of antecedents (internal and external) conditions that determine the degree of control the organization has over its environment as well as it susceptibility of crisis; (2) a typology of crisis (based on susceptibility, control, positive or negative consequences, and structural similarities) that serves as an initial crisis detection system; (3) a crisis assessment mechanism that considers the following criteria—(a) the relative threat level, (b) time restrictions, (c) the decision makers involved, (d) the quantity and quality of information, and (e) the short- and long-term implications if action is or is not taken; (4) establishment of an organization structure for managing crisis that suggests a response pattern both at the individual and organizational level; and (5) a mechanism to assess the success of solutions.

There are also characteristics that appear common to all crises:

1. Crises are determined by individual perceptions rather than objective facts.
2. Crises are often resolved during a short time frame.
3. Crises are difficult to manage because of limited control over the environment.
4. Crises in one part of an organization have implications for all other parts of the organization.

5. Crises are not inevitable.
6. Crises are not resolvable through technology or superb leadership only.
7. Internal crises are just as important as external crises.
8. Minor crises can turn into major crises, and vice versa.

Based on this review, a broader definition of crises is offered: A crisis is an event, as perceived by an individual or an aggregate; that produces some level of disruption; can be managed proactively; has negative or positive, as well as short-term or long-term implications, and is governed by a set of parameters, time, control, uncertainty, and severity.

This definition serves as the starting point for the crises management process shown in Figures 1.1 and 1.2. That is, there is a recognition in Figure 1.1 that what is perceived as a catastrophe in one business is a minor incident in another. Late delivery of certain documents may prove to be catastrophic for a local law firm, while this event has little impact on a major corporation. Consequently, all events must be considered from the "eyes of the beholder." Once level of severity is determined, the organization can then follow the management process of Figure 1.2. Any company (or individual for that matter) can employ this process. Not employing this planning process can lead to dire consequences.

INCREASE IN CRISES WORLDWIDE

This broader definition of crisis also expands the occurrence of crisis. While the airline industry, for instance, might claim that the number of crises (crashes) has declined, the number of consumer complaints has risen dramatically. Who's to say that the latter is more harmful to United Airlines than the former?

As a society we are becoming more interconnected, via the computer, satellites, and other wireless technology. This has greatly increased the complexity of relationships between the company and its various stakeholders. As a result, there are more opportunities to make mistakes; not necessarily of the catastrophic type, but certainly of the incident or accident variety. We already see evidence of this with the attempts of dot.com companies to go global. Inadequate fulfillment planning may not seem serious on a customer-by-customer basis, but added together it was sufficient to put EToys out of business. In fact, one might argue that the general disappointment of the Internet industry is not a result of major crises but thousands of minor ones, such as poor service, inadequate customer research, misleading pricing, slow delivery, and so forth.

People today have lots of choices, and a great deal more information about those choices. Consequently, it is not necessary for them to note the small problems. They simply move on to other alternatives. A company might go out of business and literally not know the cause. This is another reason why a crises planning process with a focus on monitoring crises at all levels is necessary.

RESULTS OF MISMANAGED CRISES

Undoubtedly the most serious consequence of mismanaging a crisis is the destruction of the organization. Clearly, there are less severe results. Obviously there are potential costs. Legal costs, fines and penalties, travel costs, hiring consultants, developing new materials, institutional advertisements, and communication distribution are a few examples. Lower sales and profits are also likely. Possible damage to the reputation of the company, along with a reduction of its credibility, trust, and confidence often occur. In turn, replacement of products or changing product names can result. Finally, employees may be affected by poorly managed crises. Loss of morale, reduced productivity, downsizing, and resignations have all been documented.

If we consider the negative outcomes of mismanaging a crisis from a strategic perspective, the following outcomes are likely:

- Signals of impending crises go ignored
- Crisis escapes beyond the boundary of the organization
- External stakeholders are negatively impacted
- Organization is shut down
- No learning occurs and mistakes are repeated
- Organization reputation suffers
- Organization lacks necessary resources to address crisis
- Decision making slows

The crisis in Europe cost Coca-Cola Company, the bottling company, an estimated $103 million. Further damages are difficult to assess. "It's going to take time for them to recover since all (Coca-Cola Company's) growth is overseas," says Sally Schaat, a beverage analyst with New-York based Fourteen Research. "It's tough for them because it's summer, the biggest (drink) season of the year. It still boils down to reputation, and it's going to take time to gain it back."

The situation is cogently expressed by Peter McCue, senior partner and corporate crisis management expert in the New York office of

St. Louis–based Fleischman-Hillard Inc., "Regret is the first three R's of crisis management, the other two being reform and restitution." An example of poor management is illustrated in Case 1.

THE BENEFITS OF MANAGING CRISES

Given the revised definition of crises, the situation for those companies that have no crisis management plan is depicted in Figure 1.3. Essentially, there is no process through which to identify and discern the various crises that are possible for a particular company. Instead the focus is on the most serious or immediate crises. As a result, there are no linkages between specific crises and possible disruptions created. Nor is there a mechanism for assessing positive–negative and short and long-term implications. Without this mechanism it is impossible to calculate a cost–benefit analysis for a particular crisis. That is, one cannot intelligently answer the question: Is it worth resolving this crisis?

Strategically, the benefits of properly managing a crisis are as follows:

• Signals of disruption are detected early so that the appropriate responses are brought to bear

Figure 1.3
Unplanned Crisis Model

- Major impact is confined within the organization
- Business is maintained as usual during, and after the crisis
- Lessons are applied to future disruptions
- Image of organization is maintained or even enhanced
- Organization or external stakeholders' resources are readily available for response
- Ample evidence of timely, accurate decisions, grounded in facts
- A cost–benefit analysis can be calculated

This proactive process is illustrated in Figure 1.4.

Protecting the Brand

While all the benefits listed from crisis management are important, protecting the brand stands as the most important. So what is a brand? The term "brand" comes from the ancient Norse word meaning "to burn." The original term was developed to signify the source or maker or owner of a product. From that came the more common usage, the "branding" of cattle, horses, sheep, or other possessions. As commerce developed, "brand" came to mean the origin or source of a product or to differentiate the maker from others who produce like products, such as silversmiths, china and pottery makers, leather workers, and sword makers. Today, the brand is generally used to signify or identify the manufacturer or seller of a product or service.

Today, brands occupy a unique place in commerce. Brands can be bought and sold. They can be franchised or rented. They can be

Figure 1.4
Planning for Crises

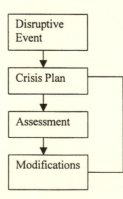

protected domestically and globally. Therefore, the brand has value to the organization, because it is a legal entity that has marketplace value other than the sales it can generate among consumers.

Brands can survive and prosper even though the products and services they represent may change significantly or disappear altogether. Brands have value, which we propose is critical to organizations today and will be increasingly so in the twenty-first century marketplace. But brands have varying values, and it is a brand's value that underpins the brand's importance. More than ownership, the brand brings marketplace meaning to the consumer. It represents what the consumer is and what he or she believes the brand provides to help reinforce his or her place in society. Thus, the brand is more than a name or a symbol or an icon—it is a relationship between the brand owner and the various stakeholders. Hurting or completely destroying that relationship is a mistake most companies cannot survive. It means the stakeholder no longer wants to be associated with that brand. What could be worse?

Necessary Steps

Putting a crisis plan in place results in a process that resembles Figure 1.3. To do this requires that the company engage the following changes:

1. Crisis planning must become an inherent part of the company's comprehensive business plan, with a focus on prevention, and the ability to calculate the cost–benefit analysis. Crisis planning is reflected by the corporate culture vis-à-vis commitment of top management, constant monitoring, and long-term investment.
2. A company must be willing to allocate adequate resources to the crisis management process. These resources incorporate all the traditional elements, including dollars, people, and time.
3. Crisis must be recast as any type of disruption, rather than a concern for catastrophic crisis only. Any minor disruption can become a catastrophe if mismanaged. Similarly, crises tend to be company specific.

CASE 1: A SHOCKED OBSERVER OR A MISSED OPPORTUNITY

After a long day, I arrived at JFK two hours early, turned in my rental car, jumped on the shuttle bus to the terminal, and realized it was the first time that I had paused all day. It had been a long trip. Still, I was able to sign several orders, and concluded my client meetings on a high note, so my fatigue was not doubled with the usual frustration of having to be on the road so many days out of the month. After finding the gate on the TV screen in the main terminal, a new novel attracted my attention in the bookstore. I was too tired to make my usual stroll around the airport, so I took the shuttle to my terminal, and positioned myself in front of Gate 37 for a pleasant period of relaxation. The relative quiet did not last long.

At 6:35 P.M. Flight 140 to San Francisco was announced for boarding. Since it wasn't my flight, I took only a passing glance at Gate 36, the origin of Flight 140. At 7:05 P.M., final boarding for that flight was announced, and five minutes later the door to Gate 36 was closed. All seemed normal for perhaps two minutes.

Then all hell broke loose. Running toward Gate 36 was a young woman, perhaps twenty-five, pushing a stroller with an infant, and dragging a two-year-old boy in tow. She was near hysteria as she reached the check-in desk. We could all hear her story, which was delivered just below a yell. Having just arrived from Germany, she was reuniting with her husband (a Sergeant in the Air Force) who she hadn't seen in nearly a month. Her children were very tired. She looked bedraggled, stressed, and about to reach her limit. I watched in amazement as the following interchange took place.

"Would you please let me board this flight?" she pleaded. "This is the last direct flight today, and I have already been traveling for almost twenty-four hours. If I don't get on this plane, I will be in serious trouble!"

The gate attendant replied, "There is no way you are getting on that plane, so there is no point in asking again." She rudely explained that she could not reopen the doors because it would be a violation of government regulations.

The young woman pleaded. The agent never changed her response. Voices were raised even higher. Everyone within one hundred yards was now focused on this melodrama. More than five minutes passed, and the gate agent made no move to help the frustrated mother and her children. She turned to her work, and pretended to ignore the desperate party. Just then, I noticed a local TV news crew that had been doing some filming in one of the duty-free shops come quickly over. The anchor told the cameraman to keep rolling, and everyone watched to see what would happen next. All eyes moved from the mother who was continuing to plead, to the children who continued to cry, to the gate agent who continued to ignore, and to the film crew that seemed ready to pounce.

Eventually the young mother noticed her plane backing from the gate. She moved to the window and began to pound on the glass and scream to all that would listen to the pain she was experiencing. Naturally, her two children matched her in emotion and volume. Anyone within ten gates of us could hear what was happening. The film crew approached. After introducing herself, the anchor asked the mother what had happened. With the camera rolling, the poor woman retold her story to sympathetic nodding and an offer to hold the baby.

After a few minutes, another ticket agent (the original agent had walked away in disgust) approached the woman and tried to steer her away from the news crew. The airline representative declined to say anything to the camera, but offered the mother and the children something to drink, and gently moved them to the airline lounge. The debacle appeared to be over.

I heard a few commiserating conversations crop up around me, people saying things like "Now I know that what I read in the paper is true: Airline customer service is horrible," and, "Makes you realize why people get so angry: That airline person didn't even try to help that poor woman." I was left sitting there thinking, How hard would it have been to call the gate agent that was still onboard, preparing the flight crew for departure? I had seen those people on almost every flight I had ever taken. And, if it really had been so impossible, why hadn't the airline employee even tried to help the mother? I made a mental note not to fly this airline again if possible, because I certainly did not want to be treated the way that poor woman had. I wondered what would happen after the story appeared on the news that night, and returned to my book.

Observations

- Even though this event would not be considered a catastrophe for an airline, there is little doubt that the event produced immediate and long-term negative consequences. Showing empathy on a day-to-day basis may prove just as important as a response to a crash.

- As the almost instantaneous appearance of the press shows, you never know when you will get bad press. If employees have guidelines that help them avoid major problems every day, then hopefully on the day the news crew shows up, they will have had lots of practice.

CONCLUSION

Unlike other books and papers that have addressed the notion of crisis management, the approach taken in this book differs in several important ways. Most notably, it rejects the notion that the only crises worth considering and managing are the catastrophes prevalent with major companies. Instead, crisis management is important to businesses of all sizes, for-profit and not-for-profit, and both those crisis prone and not crisis prone. The planning model described in the following pages is adaptable to all businesses. Implementing the model does not guarantee that bad things won't happen to your company. It does, however, guarantee that the number of crises will be reduced and/or the results will be less disruptive.

The next chapter covers the topic of marketing research, a skill necessary for crisis management.

2

The Activity of Doing Research

When you come to a fork in the road, take it.

Yogi Berra

Connecticut will receive $3.6 billion from the national tobacco settlement over the next five years. Jerry Wigand, former vice president for research at Brown & Williamson Tobacco Corporation, says despite the settlement (national tobacco settlement of $206 billion), tobacco companies continue to mislead the public about their product. He says tobacco companies falsify the amounts of nicotine and tar in their product by measuring the level produced when a cigarette is smoked by a machine rather than a person.

The industry denies that. Seth Moskowitz, a spokesman for RJ Reynolds Tobacco Holdings Inc., says the federal government, not the tobacco companies, came up with the test for tar and nicotine. Moskowitz says the settlement will result in a lot of changes. "The master settlement agreement comprehensively addressed the major issues concerning cigarette marketing and youth smoking in the U.S.," he says. "It has put in place a number of bans as well as severe restrictions and has fundamentally changed the way cigarettes can be marketed."

As a citizen of the world you have to answer a very basic question about the tobacco industry: Do you believe the industry did or did not intentionally sell a product that could prove lethal to its customers? Recent results suggest that over 80 percent of those surveyed believe the tobacco industry did produce a lethal product. Although no one knows the exact cost in dollars and human misery caused by this product, we do know that it represents one of the greatest catastrophes in human history. There have been millions of victims; including smokers, medical insurance providers, retailers, farmers, the media, and family members, to name a few. Some are affected in a very serious way, others hardly at all. In every instance, each of these victims and quasi-victims could have utilized the planning process delineated in this book.

Research is the backbone of crisis management. It provides the factual foundation for marketing intelligent crisis-related decisions. We have already delineated many facts associated with research on crisis management. However, it is always tenuous to accept someone else's research findings as fact; particularly if you are not familiar with the research process. This is not to suggest that reading this chapter will somehow make you a research expert. However, it will introduce you to several key concepts and suggest the parameters associated with doing research.

INTUITION

The intelligent strategy decision in crisis management is based on both knowledge and understanding of the crisis situation. Understanding can come in a variety of forms. A manager who has worked in an industry for twenty-five years may have an intuitive understanding of how the business operates—plus a head full of facts about the situation at hand. Past experience provides expertise. Someone who has tried various techniques knows from experience what works and what doesn't.

This intuitive understanding and experience-based wisdom are the bases for many strategy decisions. In fact, some corporate executives believe that experience is the best basis for a decision. But even people who have been intimately involved in a business for years sometimes fail to understand what is happening with their industry, their company, or individuals impacted by the company.

SYSTEMATIC RESEARCH

Research is a more systematic way to acquire information and to gain an intelligent viewpoint. Although it is particularly useful for people who do not have twenty-five years experience, it can also provide surprising information to experienced managers. Many executives have discovered they were running blind before a systematic research effort was undertaken to answer a question or investigate a problem.

THE RESEARCH MODEL

Research remains one of the most misunderstood and maligned activities in all of business. Maybe it goes back to our youth when a common response to an elementary teacher was "I'm just no good at math!" The world was divided into two basic groups—those that like numbers and the rest of us. The former grew up to be scientists, engineers, investment bankers, accountants, and computer nerds. Some even became interested in doing business research.

Since large companies tend to outsource the research function and small companies tend to skip it altogether, the intent of this chapter is to simply introduce you to the basics. It is just enough information so that you can understand how useful research is in managing crisis. The process is illustrated in Figure 2.1.

Figure 2.1
The Research Model

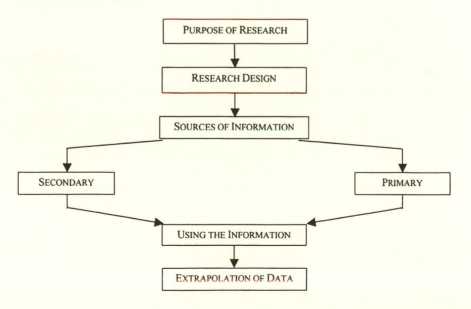

Research Objectives

In carrying out crisis analysis and planning, managers need information at almost every turn. In today's rapidly changing environments, managers also need more up-to-date information to make timely decisions. Yet managers frequently complain that they lack enough information of the right kind or have too much of the wrong kind. One source of this problem is the manager's inability or unwillingness to establish research objectives.

The manager and researcher must work closely together to define the research problem carefully and agree on research objectives. The manager best understands the problem or decision for which the information is needed; the researcher best understands the research process and how to obtain the information. Managers must know enough about research to help in the planning and to interpret research results. If they know little about research, they may obtain the wrong information, accept wrong conclusions, or ask for information that costs too much. Experienced researchers who understand the manager's problem should also be involved at this stage. The researcher must be able to help the manager define the problem and to suggest ways that research can help the manager make better decisions.

Defining the problem and research objectives is often the hardest step in the research process. The manager may know that something is wrong, but not the specific causes. For example, managers of a discount retail chain store hastily decided that falling sales were caused by poor advertising and ordered research to test the company's advertising. When this research showed that the current advertising was reaching the right people with the right message, the managers were puzzled. It turned out the stores themselves were not providing what the advertising promised. More careful problem definition would have avoided the cost and delay of doing the research. It would have suggested research on the real problem.

Finally, the following questions are helpful in delineating the research objectives:

- What information do you want?
- How will you use this information?
- Who (or what) should we study?
- What should we ask them (or what should we measure)?
- How much can we pay for the research?
- When do we need the results?

Will the research be used to influence anyone other than yourself or your department?

Research Design

When the problem has been carefully defined and research objectives developed, the researcher must next determine the research design. Research designs are general strategies or plans of action for addressing the research problem, the data collection, and the analysis process. The problem definition stage is likely to suggest approaches for determining which research design to use. Research generally has three purposes: exploration, description, or solution. They result in three general types of research design: exploratory, descriptive, and causal.

Exploratory research is typically carried out to satisfy the researcher's desire for better understanding, or to develop preliminary background and suggest issues for a more detailed follow-up study. Exploratory research can be conducted using literature reviews, case analyses, interviews, and focus groups. Better understanding of a problem might begin with a review of prior research. This might entail a review of similar companies and identification of the types of crises they faced, and how they dealt with them. Collecting books and articles on crisis management might also be part of the literature review. (Please refer to the end of the book where you will find a list of suggested readings.) In-depth interviews with individuals who already have some knowledge of the problem(s) may also prove helpful.

Descriptive research is normally directed by one or more formal research questions or hypotheses. Typically, a survey or questionnaire is administered to a sample from a population of interest to the firm, such as customers who file complaints against your company. Descriptive studies may be cross-sectional or longitudinal, depending on the timing of the observation. For example, a survey of customers administered at a given time to assess perceived satisfaction with a particular service is a cross-sectional study. Customers who participate in panel studies of purchase behavior over a period of time are involved in longitudinal research.

Exploratory and descriptive studies can help answer certain questions, but identification of cause and effect relationships require causal research. Causal designs call for experiments in which researchers manipulate independent variables and then observe or measure the dependent variable or variable of interest. Suppose that a company wants to assess what level of price increase would prove acceptable to their customers. To test this, the company matches three markets, using key demographics, product sales, and market size. In one market, the product has a $1.99 price, in the second the price was $2.49, and in the third, a $2.99 price was charged. At the end of the experiment, the company compares sales in the three markets and learns that the $2.49 price generates more sales.

Data Types

Recall from Figure 1.2 that research provides input at each stage of the crisis management process. Essentially, research can be derived from two sources of information—secondary and primary.

Secondary Research

The first step in any research effort is to review information that is already available, whether from the company's own historical records or from syndicated or library sources. This is secondary research. It should always come first so that you and your colleagues can start at the right place in terms of designing the rest of your research process.

Sources of Secondary Research

There are a number of information sources available to the business planner. As we sort through material, we must look for anything that might help us better understand managing business crises.

Company records or company intelligence. The amount of information that is gathered and stored by a company and that can be useful to the crisis planner is amazing. Fortunately, many companies in today's marketplace recognize the value of such data and are making an effort to house them in accessible databases. The key to obtaining and using existing company information is a clear, concise description of what is needed and in what form it is needed. If the needed information can be adequately described to the accounting or financial people, it usually can be obtained. Examples of such information particularly germane to crisis planners might be sales, product returns, employee turnover, and slow payment.

Previous company research. In many cases, a great deal of information can be taken from studies conducted by the company for reasons other than crisis management. This information may consist of consumer data, product tests, distribution information, and priority tests. In some instances, the information may be held in the marketing department; in others, it may be found in a research department or even the human resources department, or others.

Trade and association studies. Many trade journals and associations conduct surveys of their readers and collect data about their particular field or industry as part of an ongoing service. Many trade associations develop quite sophisticated data and information for their members. In many specialized or limited fields or activities, the trade association may be the only source of useful information.

Census and/or registration data. One of the most overlooked sources of information is the data developed or gathered by various government organizations. Federal, state, and local governments are particularly good sources of data on almost any subject. The federal government publishes information through the Census Bureau on such topics as population, housing, retail trade, wholesale trade, service industries, manufacturers, agriculture, and transportation. Virtually any large library can provide most of the census data; in addition, the Census Bureau Web site, http://www.census.gov, contains a wealth of easily searchable information. Because new census material is constantly being published, a thorough study of existing information should be made before additional research is undertaken.

Libraries and universities. The library can quickly become one of the crisis planner's best friends. Magazine and newspaper articles can be the source of important information on market trends and competitive activity. The search process is easier today than it has ever been, thanks to CD-ROM technology. There are a number of business information databases available, including ABI-Inform, Info-track, Dow Jones News/Retrieval, NEXIS, Wilson Businessdisk, and Compact Disclosure. And the consumer press can also be included in the search; the *Reader's Guide to Periodical Literature* is another available on-line information source. Most of these services operate in the same way: The researcher types in a key word or words (such as a company name, product name, or subject), and the system searches the database for criterion containing that word. The computer generates a list of citations, which may contain an abstract of the article in addition to the author, title, source, and date.

The Internet. Today, the Internet and the World Wide Web are many researchers' first steps on a hunt for information. Many companies maintain Web sites that provide background information on their products and services. In addition, there are Web sites dedicated to helping searchers find information, such as the Virtual Reference Desk at http://thorplus.lib.purdue.edu/reference/index.html and Research It! at http://www.itools.com/research-it/research-it.html. Simple searches using mainstream search engines such as Yahoo, AltaVista, and Google can also yield a wealth of information. The benefit of starting with the Internet when beginning your research is the relative speed with which you can browse for names of individuals, names of companies, the topics of crisis, management, and marketing themselves, and the "unauthorized" sites that will also emerge in addition to those that are authorized.

Measures of reported and actual behavior. Two major sources of syndicated secondary data on consumer behavior are the Simmons Research Bureau (SMRB) and Mediamark Research, Inc. (MRI). Both companies deal with reported behavior; that is, they gather data annually through extensive consumer surveys in which respondents are asked about their geographic and demographic characteristics, buying behavior, and media usage behavior. Both companies make their data available in both multivolume book and CD-ROM formats. There is one important point to keep in mind with SMRB and MRI: The data are based on self-reports. The participating consumer fills out a booklet with page after page of questions. Obviously, there's some potential for confusion in the reporting.

To avoid human error problems (as well as lack of truthfulness) in research, the crisis planner can sometimes go to the source: records of actual purchase, product usage behavior, consumer complaints, returned products, employee turnover and accidents, and so forth. The best source for such information is the company's own database. But if the planner does not have a database, or has recently started to develop one, there are other sources of actual behavioral data. For example, in the realm of consumer information, the following would be good choices: Information Resources, Inc. (IRI) at http://www.infores.com gathers a wide variety of purchasing data; Database America at http://www.databaseamerica.com is one of a number of companies that collects information from a number of sources and then makes that compiled data available to marketers to match against the consumers in their own database; Claritas at http://www.claritas.com offers a number of products, the best known is PRIZM, a market segmentation system that places every U.S. neighborhood into one of sixty-two clusters defined on the basis of demographics, psychographics, and behavior.

Locating these data and determining their accuracy are the major obstacles to their use. The information (not including information collected by the government) has been gathered for a purpose and usually been funded by some organization. Care should be taken in analyzing the data-gathering method, sample size, and age of the information when it is being used for a research base. Case 2 illustrates the results of secondary research.

CASE 2: FEAR OF FLYING

In 1998 the death rate on U.S. air carriers was zero; by contrast, over that same Thanksgiving weekend, 598 people died on U.S. highways. And yet, even as the industry nightly touts its safety record, the "unfriendly skies" have increasingly become a source of lesser horror stories.

As we move farther into the jet age, when even mid-level professionals fly regularly for work, air travel has come to feel increasingly onerous. In a recent *Newsweek* poll, more than half of adult fliers said they were sometimes frightened when they flew; in 1983, only one-third said this. Citing safety concerns, 34 percent said they avoid certain airlines, up from just 19 percent in 1983. And nearly one-quarter said they "avoid flying whenever they can." Anxiety, too, is up: 43 percent said flying has become "more stressful" in recent years.

In the first nine months of 1999, the Department of Transportation received almost 16,000 complaints from air travelers (the department estimates that for every complaint it receives, the airline gets 400). Complaints center around issues such as arbitrary ticket prices, endless delays, bad food, cramped seating, stale air, dirty planes, lost luggage, and rude service.

OBSERVATION

* It appears there's a great deal of negative information collected about commercial flying. Surely there must be positive information. Think about these possibilities as well, along with possible extrapolation.

Types of Primary Research

Even the most thorough review of secondary information often leaves questions unanswered, particularly in terms of crisis management issues. When this is the case, the planner needs to supplement the secondary information with primary research. Primary research is original research carried out to gather specific information about the problem being studied.

No matter which type of primary research is used, data are usually gathered either by observation or by survey research. In observation data gathering, people are observed as they engage in a variety of behaviors, such as shopping, using a product, or otherwise involved with the company and its products or services. Survey data gathering entails asking a number of people about their attitudes, beliefs, and behaviors around a particular issue.

There is also a relationship between qualitative and exploratory research. Qualitative research is undertaken when the information needed is directional or diagnostic. Such research is usually done with fairly small groups of people, and the sampling is conducted on a quota or availability basis. Definitive conclusions usually cannot be drawn from qualitative research. Instead, an attempt is made to get a general impression of the situation or issue. Qualitative research is often used in conjunction with exploratory research. Exploratory research represents the initial stages in answering a research question. In some instances, its purpose may be to identify the correct problem. Common research techniques employed in exploratory research are focus groups, depth interviews, and projective techniques. A focus group is a discussion group made up of six to ten members of the target group for the problem of interest. A trained moderator guides the group members through a discussion of a series of issues. The depth interview is conducted in a way similar to the focus group, except that interviews are done on an individual basis. All projective techniques have the same basic approach: the person being interviewed is asked to involve himself or herself in a situation or experience in which he or she projects feelings and experiences about issues set up by the interviewer.

Quantitative or descriptive research. Quantitative or descriptive research usually is primary research. The results can be projected to various portions of the universe, and the laws of statistical probability can be applied to lend support to, or cause rejection of, the findings. Whereas qualitative research is used primarily to give direction to the crisis planner, quantitative research is used most often in choosing between alternatives or in decision making. The two most common methods used to gather quantitative data are observation and survey.

Observational research. The activities or habits of persons are observed either personally or through some mechanical means, such as with scanner panels or video. Historical data are gathered according to what the given person was observed doing or had done in the past: The data are used both to assess past behavior (and the reasons for it) and to predict future behavior. Observations can be very helpful to the crisis planner. However, collecting enough observations to generate conclusive answers to research questions can be quite an expensive undertaking.

Ethnographic research. This method attempts to record how people actually use products and services in day-to-day activity. This form of direct observation—called *ethnography*—is based on techniques borrowed from sociology and anthropology. For example, a researcher may actually enter the customer's home, observe consumption behavior, and record pantry and even garbage content. This method of collecting more realistic data has increased dramatically.

Survey research. This is the most common method of primary research data gathering used in business. As the name implies, data are obtained through a survey of individuals. The usual goal is to obtain information necessary to develop a profile of the individuals' behaviors, attitudes, and opinions. Survey research methodologies differ according to the method of data gathering employed. The most common forms are personal interviews, mail surveys, panels, and telephone interviews. The Internet is increasingly being employed to do survey research.

Data-Gathering Techniques

As noted, there are five data-gathering techniques most commonly issued in marketing research. A personal interview implies a direct face-to-face conversation between the interviewer and the respondent. The interview can take place in a home or office or at a central location like a mall where shoppers are stopped or intercepted and asked to participate. This technique probably provides the highest and most targeted response rate. It also provides the greatest flexibility in that questions can be reworded, reordered, or clarified. However, this technique is the most expensive in that it requires well-trained, well-paid interviewers, close supervision, and various set-up costs. It is also subject to interviewer bias.

The telephone interview means that the conversation occurs over the phone. In all these cases, the interviewer asks the questions and records the respondent's answers either while the interview is in progress or immediately afterward. This method is fast to administer and complete and relatively inexpensive. It requires little supervision if the training is adequate. However, it is often difficult to derive accurate call lists, plus there's no guarantee that you are speaking to the right person. Finally, the interview must be short and there's no assurance that the respondent won't hang-up half way through the interview or lie.

The mail questionnaire is sent to designated respondents with an accompanying cover letter. The respondents complete the questionnaire and mail their replies back to the research organization. This technique allows for flexibility on the respondent's part and provides for a lengthy questionnaire, often including sensitive questions. There is also no interviewer bias. It is also relatively inexpensive. The limitations are quite real. Most notably, you cannot control the response time or who actually answered the questionnaire. There is no capability for explaining confusing questions, probing, or making sure the questionnaire is completely answered.

The panel is a fixed group of respondents that may include stores, dealers, individuals, or other entities. The members of the panel are surveyed on a regular basis. Panels can be an excellent way of measuring change over time. It also allows the researcher to use a variety of questions, including the diary method. Panels can be very targeted, representing the exact people of interest. Unfortunately, panels are expensive to establish and maintain. Replacing dropouts is not always easy. Finally, panels have high burnout.

On-line surveys are now a viable means of collecting the opinions of people, according to a recent research study conducted by Digital Marketing Services (DMS). The survey found that many of the same people using traditional forms of marketing research are now using on-line surveys, yet on-line surveys are also capturing those no longer willing to participate in other survey methods. Marketers are now recognizing the validity of the on-line medium and reaping the benefits that on-line surveys provide by gathering data faster and more cost effectively while providing an easier and more convenient means for the consumer.

There are also criticisms of this on-line technology. They argue that Internet surveys combine relatively low response rates with self-selection bias. Also, a growing body of anecdotal and hard evidence suggests that while people might be interested in the first Internet interview that they see and therefore are more likely to respond, the novelty quickly erodes.

Sampling for Data Gathering

The success of any research effort depends on the sample selected for data gathering. The major objective is to make sure that respondents to be interviewed are representative of the entire target population. It is important to determine who is to be sampled, the procedure to be used for sample selection, and the size of the sample. Identifying the persons to be interviewed or observed is creating the sample frame. If the crisis planner wants to learn about excessive complaints from a particular retail outlet, for example, then customers shopping at that outlet should be considered. Those who do not shop there would not be included in the study.

There are two basic sampling techniques. Probability samples are those in which every known unit in the universe has a known probability of being selected for the study. For example, if the universe were defined as Dairy Queen outlets in the city of Omaha, Nebraska, with sales exceeding $500,000 annually, a complete list of stores meeting this criteria could be developed. If twenty-seven such stores were identified then each store has a one in twenty-seven chance of being selected. The results from research conducted using a probability sample can be projected to the larger population from which the sample was drawn.

A nonprobability sample does not provide every unit in the universe with a known chance of being included in the sample frame. If, in the earlier example, the restrictions might be relaxed from Dairy Queen stores doing over $500,000 in sales in Omaha to simply those located within easy access to major highways, this would not be a probability sample. Although the results cannot be projected to the larger population, nonprobability samples are widely used in business research because no listing of the complete universe is available in many categories. Also, the sampling technique is much less costly, in terms of both time and money.

There are a number of alternatives under the nonprobability sampling category. Convenience samples, also called accidental samples, are composed of people who enter the study by accident, in that they just happen to be where the information for the study is being collected. Examples of convenience samples abound in our everyday lives. We talk to a few friends, and on the basis of their reactions, we infix the political sentiment of the country; our local radio station asks people to call in and express their reactions to some controversial issue, and the opinions expressed are interpreted as prevailing sentiment. The problem with convenience samples, of course, is that we have no way of knowing if those included are representative of the target population.

Another type of nonprobability sample is called judgment or purposive sampling. Most typically, the sample elements are selected because it is believed that they are representative of the population of interest. One example of a judgment sample is seen every four years at presidential election time, when television viewers are treated to in-depth analyses of the serving communities. These communities are thought to be representative, since in previous elections the local winner has been the president. Thus, by monitoring these pivotal communities, election analysts are able to offer an early prediction of the eventual winner. As long as the researcher is at the early stages of research when ideas or insights are being sought—when the researcher realizes their limitations—the judgment sample can be used productively. It becomes dangerous, though, when it is employed in descriptive or causal studies and its weaknesses are conveniently forgotten.

A third type of nonprobability sample, the quota sample, attempts to be representational of the population by including the same proportion of elements possessing a certain characteristic as is found in the population. Consider for example, an attempt to select a representative sample of undergraduate students on a college campus. If the eventual sample of 500 contained no seniors, one would have serious reservations about the representativeness of the sample and the generalizability of the conclusions beyond the immediate sample group. With a quota sample, the researcher could ensure that seniors would be included and in the same proportion as they occur in the entire undergraduate student body. There are several potential problems with quota samples. First, the sample could be very far off with respect to some other important characteristic likely to influence the result. Also, it is difficult to verify whether a quota sample is representative. Finally, interviewers who are left to their own devices are prone to follow certain practices, sometimes biased.

In a probability sample, researchers can calculate the likelihood that any given population element will be included, because the final sample elements are selected objectively by a specific process and not according to the whims of the researcher or field worker. Since the elements are selected objectively, researchers are then able to assess the reliability of the sample results, something not possible with nonprobability samples regardless of the careful judgment exercised in selecting individuals.

Simple random sampling is the most common type of probability sampling. In a simple random sample, each unit-included in the sample has a known and equal chance of being selected for study, and every combination of population elements is a sample possibility. For example, if we wanted a simple random sample of all students enrolled in a particular college, we might assign a number to each student on a comprehensive list of all those enrolled and then have a computer pick a sample randomly.

One of the most difficult tasks in planning or evaluating primary research is determining the sample size required to achieve a given level of confidence. Statistical techniques are available for developing confidence levels of probability samples. The problem becomes more complex with nonprobability studies because the true universe usually is unknown. A number of rules of thumb exist that are helpful to the crisis planner for determining sample sizes. In intensive data gathering, such as depth interviews or focus groups, most ideas concerning an issue will be verbalized after the first thirty or so persons have been interviewed. Similarly, interviews with 100–200 people, given a standard questionnaire in a limited geographic area, will tend to indicate the general attitudes of the population. For a regional study including several cities or a few states, a sample of 300–400 qualified respondents is normally considered to be sufficient. A sample of 1,000–2,000 qualified subjects, selected according to a probability sample will generally reflect the questions and feelings of the national population on most subjects.

Using the Information

Information gathering is only the first step in the research process. The second and much more critical step in using the information is to make crisis management decisions. In each of the chapters that follow, there will be illustrations of the types of inferences that may be drawn from the data collected through research.

Extrapolation of Data

Although it is often true that data often exist for issues currently being considered, and that the real task is to determine what data are needed and how they might be gathered, this is not always the case. For example, even though a company has experienced very little turnover of top management, the crisis planner may note that most of these individuals are approximately the same age, and will be retiring within the same five-year period. This is where the crisis planner must get creative and develop a new strategy for top management. This may entail examining case studies of companies facing a similar problem, interviewing current mid-level managers, interviewing current top managers about their retirement plans, and so forth. This technique of converting existing data into usable information for another area is called data extrapolation. The extrapolation of data is limited only by the ability and creativity of the person seeking the information.

THE COST OF RESEARCH

Be forewarned that doing research can be a very expensive proposition, ranging into the hundreds of thousands of dollars. As noted earlier, it is critical to assess what you know about your company and its situation, and what you don't know. Often the high cost of doing research is a result of collecting information you already have or don't need. Of course, doing the research may prove that what you thought you knew was incorrect. There's always the possibility that senior management at a company may not value research because "they know the business inside and out." Such knowledge, while valuable, may prove inadequate when managing crises. The key is to find the right balance between doing just enough research to validate what you know—and find out what you don't know as well.

The old adage, "you get what you pay for" is not always valid when applied to business research. Like bad physicians, lawyers, and auto mechanics, the price charged does not always correlate with quality. Shop around. Ask friends and colleagues about their experiences with various research firms. If you're in a college town, contact the statistics and/or the marketing departments. Sometimes your research needs can be met by a class project—often, absolutely free. Consider contacting faculty. They don't have the overhead of research firms. Once you find someone who is willing to commit to learning about your business and its issues, and provides high quality and objective information, as MasterCard says, "they're priceless."

CONCLUSION

Providing company decision makers with good information is good business. This information is necessary for effective crisis management. Knowing how to do business research in-house or outsourcing the task is a prerequisite for businesses of all sizes. If you don't have these skills, acquire them—or find someone who does.

3

Assessing Your Vulnerability

If you can't keep your head when all about you are losing theirs,
it's just possible you haven't grasped the situation.
Humorist Jean Kerr

The relative calm of 4:20 A.M. on a Saturday in Cleveland was shattered (literally) by a water-main break at the corner of Superior Avenue and East 12th Street. Suddenly, forty-pound chunks of asphalt were launched through office building windows, trailed by a million gallons of water. The below-freezing air temperature added a surreal Winter Carnival quality, as icicles quickly spangled the windows and outer walls of the building and turned the office carpeting into an ice rink. The floors affected were the second, third, and fourth, the main lobby at street level, and all below-ground offices. The water in the basement rose to between two and three feet in depth, and on the upper floors to eight inches deep.

As water flooded the fourth floor, it soaked through the carpeting, flooring, and ceiling of the third floor, which also was already flooded and compounded the problem on the already-flooded second floor. Then it froze. Saturated ceiling tiles crumbled and fell, spilling water and debris onto computer equipment, desktops, and chairs. Drywall between offices warped or collapsed. File cabinets filled with water, their sides warped and the paint peeled from them. The electricity had long since shorted out, causing data not properly saved on computers to be lost. Advertising film negatives on production managers' desks became "negative sandwiches," glued together by the debris-filled water. Paper documents fused to each other and to surfaces, and resin-coated stock began to deteriorate immediately. Damage was estimated at $2 to $3 million.

Miraculously, nobody was injured—but were the businesses in the facility mortally wounded? In fact, many of the building's tenants were devastated by the accident. Furnishings, files, and other important documents were destroyed. However, the major tenant, Penton Publishing, survived quite nicely. In Penton's case, its new disaster recovery plan—completed just a few months before the water-main break—had the company up and running within hours after the disaster, and operating at full power within two weeks. Notes Susan Grimm, vice president of publishing support services at Penton, "Last year, we used REXSYS disaster recovery software to build a database of basic recovery plans and phone numbers of vendors and employees on disaster recovery teams. . . . The teams got down to work and did exactly what they were supposed to do. Now we will update the plan with what we learned from this experience, and we'll get plans in place for our other offices."

The disaster may have even produced positive outcomes. Said Penton Publishing's President Dan Ramella, "The flood accelerated our plan for upgrading our technology. Instead of phasing gradually into it, we were shoved into it. The result has been outstanding. . . . Our disaster plan worked to perfection. I couldn't be more proud of the way our people pitched in to do whatever was asked of them, regardless of what it was."

Clearly, the proactive approach Penton Publishing took to manage potential crises is admirable. Essentially, they addressed the traditional question asked in crisis management: "What is the worst thing that could happen to my business?" In the case of a magazine publisher the answer is fairly straightforward: "All my work and supportive materials will be lost." Consequently, all the crisis prevention efforts were focused on saving this work. The type of catastrophe was irrelevant. Whether it was a fire, earthquake, flood, or computer hacker; the system's purpose was to save the work.

Fortunately, no one was hurt in the accident. But what if people had been injured, or even killed? Would the employees still rally to get the company up and running? Their perceptions of the incident, how it was handled by management, what they felt was expected of them would have been different if their colleagues had indeed been killed. Were the employees rewarded for their efforts? It was later noticed that several hundred boxes full of materials were on the floor and this material was irretrievable. Did someone know what was in them?

The intent here is not to discount the efforts of Penton Publishing. They effectively dealt with the major crisis, and that is appropriate. However, they did not have a strategy in place (my assumption) to deal with the whole range of other possible disruptions. Quite a lot was left to chance.

The basic premise in this book is that all disruptions (crises) faced by a company are important. Since crises are perceived by individuals based on their own set of criteria, what appears to be a minor crisis to one person may be considered a disaster by someone else. For example, the death of the CEO at Presido Steel is sad, but not a crisis; while the death of Martha Stewart would be a true catastrophe to her company.

The first stage in the decision model presented in Figure 1.2 was for the firm to assess their crisis situation. In this chapter we present this process. It involves three separate analyses:

1. an assessment of the strategic management process
2. the development of a general crisis classification
3. the conducting of a crisis audit for a particular company

THE STRATEGIC MANAGEMENT PROCESS

In this section we develop a strategically anchored model of crisis management that builds on the collective strength and wisdom of previous frameworks, and propose a crisis classification matrix useful to all businesses. Both lay the foundation for identifying the specific crises faced by a particular business. Essentially, crisis managers will be able to base the rest of their crisis management plan on the outcome of this classification process.

The review of the crisis literature delineated in Chapter 1 suggests that crises are differentiated from more routine strategic decisions by their attendant time pressures, control issues, threat-level concerns, and response-option constraints. As portrayed in Figure 3.1, crisis management is first and foremost a strategic problem. Resolution requires that managers actually confront the six major tasks identified as comprising strategic management:

1. environmental analysis
2. goal formulation

Figure 3.1
Crisis Management Strategic Considerations

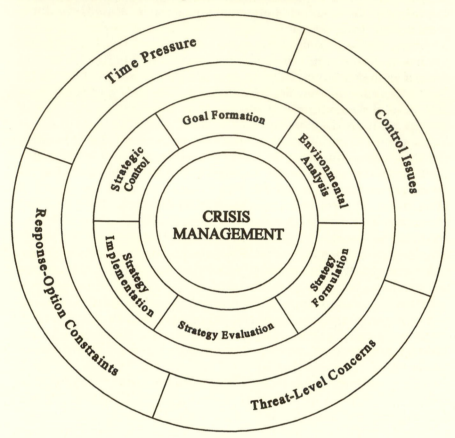

3. strategy formulation
4. strategy evaluation
5. strategy implementation
6. strategic control

Unfortunately, and as the outer ring in Figure 3.1 indicates, crises inhibit the strategic management process in four specific ways.

Unlike normal business plans, which may be updated over a one- or two-year period, crises often require immediate action. Such time pressure severely limits the attention managers can give to each of the six major strategic management tasks. For example, as word of the Tylenol poisonings spread in 1982, Johnson & Johnson felt compelled to act quickly and decisively. Their management was forced to evaluate the complex implications attached to product recall in a matter of days, something that under normal conditions would be given months of scrutiny. A much less dramatic example affected by time pressure might be a delay of employee paychecks due to a computer malfunction. For employees expecting their pay on the fourth Tuesday of the month, a delay to Thursday is not acceptable, and the company has serious time pressure to resolve this disruption immediately.

A second inhibiting characteristic of a crisis relates to control. For illustrative purposes, consider the leveraged buyout of Federated Department Stores by Campeau in 1988. Able to raise the necessary capital, Campeau left Federated's management team with little, if any, control over the organization's destiny. The same lack of control would prevail when a female employee (not at Federated), three months pregnant, was exposed to asbestos fiber from a floor being remodeled nearby. Whether the infant was harmed was unknown for several months. A more typical control problem is how the media responds to problems experienced by an organization.

Crises also create threats that vary in their magnitude and severity. From a strategic management perspective, threat-level concerns pose unique and often insurmountable challenges to the strategy formulation, strategy evaluation, and strategy implementation tasks. The decision by A. H. Robbins in the late 1970s to continue marketing the Dalcon Shield, for example, clearly illustrates how difficult it is to both define and predict threat levels. Although they did not know it at the time, this decision would initially lead to negative public relations, followed by large numbers of law suits, Chapter 11 bankruptcy, and ultimately, acquisition by another company. Likewise, what appears at first to be a simple sexual-harassment suit, may be picked up by a major news service and become devastating to the company. Minor disruptions can turn into major catastrophes.

A fourth inhibiting characteristic of crises relates to response-option constraints. Consider the situation faced by Johnson & Johnson in 1986. Although package security had been improved on all Tylenol products since the first poisoning in 1982, a second incident involving capsules in 1986 left Johnson & Johnson with few response options. Confronting a loss in consumer confidence for the second time in four years, Johnson & Johnson had little choice but to halt the production of Tylenol in capsule form. The same limited response options would prevail for a local restaurant that discovered three of their patrons experienced food poisoning. Refunding the cost of the meal, paying medical expenses, and providing a coupon for free future meals would likely be a minimum response.

In summary, crisis management requires a sensitivity to strategic management fundamentals. Proper identification of a crisis is a critically important first step and requires that environmental analysis and goal formulation tasks are undertaken. Management activity confronts the crisis when formulating and evaluating their strategic options. Finally, the tasks of strategy implementation and strategic control require that the organization reconfigure itself through the deployment of resources. This consolidated view of the strategic management process is exacerbated during a crisis by time pressures, control issues, threat-level concerns, and response-option constraints.

THE CRISIS CLASSIFICATION MATRIX

Classification has played a traditionally important role in the evaluation of business. Classification is valuable because it simplifies complex structures, helps to organize the collection of information, provides diagnostic insights, and has the potential to facilitate improvements in strategic planning. Also, as noted earlier, such a classification can serve as the basis for crisis planning.

The four distinguishing characteristics of a crisis highlighted in Figure 3.1 provide an excellent basis for classifying strategic problems. As shown in Figure 3.2, problem events (disruptions) can be classified in a sixteen-cell matrix, based on threat level (high ver-

Figure 3.2
Crisis Classification Matrix

Threat Level \ Time Pressure		Intense		Minimal	
Response Options \ Degree of Control		Low	High	Low	High
Low	Many	(4) Level 2	(3) Level 1	(2) Level 1	(1) Level 0
	Few	(8) Level 3	(7) Level 2	(6) Level 2	(5) Level 1
High	Many	(12) Level 3	(11) Level 2	(10) Level 2	(9) Level 1
	Few	(16) Level 4	(15) Level 3	(14) Level 3	(13) Level 2

sus low), response options (few versus many), time pressure (intense versus minimal), and degree of control (high versus low). While the most challenging problems are found in the lone level four cell where the time pressure is intense, the degree of control is low, the threat level is high, and response options are few in number; problems that would certainly be classified as traditional crises can also be found in level two and level three cells. In these cells, two or three of the characteristics that differentiate severe disruptions from more routine strategic decisions are inhibiting the strategic management process. Problems found in level one cells, as well as the lone level zero cell, would be classified as minor disruptions. A hypothetical set of disruptions are identified in some of the cells so as to illustrate how level zero, level one, level two, level three, and level four disruptions differ from one another (see Figure 3.3). This classification somewhat parallels the crisis continuum introduced in Chapter 1.

Use of the crisis classification matrix has the potential to provide organizations with a variety of strategic benefits. The process of simultaneously classifying strategic problems in a four dimensional matrix according to their threat level, time pressure, degree of control, and response-option constraints also provides numerous crisis management benefits. For example, just as the "BCG Growth–Share Matrix" lets management know that a strategic business unit classified as a problem child will need substantial influx of cash to

Figure 3.3
Crisis Classification Matrix with Examples

Threat Level / Response Options / Degree of Control	Time Pressure → Intense		Minimal	
	Low	High	Low	High
Low — Many		Officer Scandal		Customer Complaint
Low — Few	Strike	Stock Decline	Sexual Harassment Suit	
High — Many	Floods	Intel Pentium chip	CEO Retirement	
High — Few	Jack in the Box E-coli	Tylenol	Exxon Valdez	Proctor & Gamble Logo Rumor

increase its market share in a growing market, the crises classification matrix improves decision making by doing the following: (1) displaying in one location the array of strategic problems that must be (or might need to be) confronted, (2) providing a basis for the establishment of priorities, and (3) aiding in the deployment of managerial and financial resources. Clearly, the classification also facilitates the next phase of the crisis assessment process—customizing it for your organization.

A PERSONALIZED CRISIS AUDIT

The personalized classification process requires that analysis precede classification, that background support classification, and that alternative solutions directly relate to the crisis identified. All these tasks strengthen problem-solving skills and help make crisis managers more strategic in their orientation.

Doing a personalized crisis audit is a three-step process:

1. Create a susceptibility index.
2. Create a probability index.
3. Complete the classification matrix.

Create a Susceptibility Index

Every organization is more or less susceptible to a variety of disruptions (crises). Airlines, power plants, and chemical plants may be considered the most susceptible to major catastrophes, often resulting in loss of lives. Other businesses, such as fast food stores and retail outlets are vulnerable to milder disruptions such as employee turnover, spoiled food, or long lines. Moreover, these susceptibilities can change over time. Many universities, for example, are facing the inevitable crisis that a large percent of their faculty will be retiring during a five-year period of time, starting in approximately 2005. Some are preparing for this crisis, others are not. Correcting a crisis should mean that susceptibility is reduced.

The following is a partial list of crises that can strike any business:

- Employee layoffs or downsizing
- Lawsuits
- Poor financial performance
- Discrimination, harassment claims or charges
- Negative media coverage
- Damaging rumors

- Product defects or quality problems
- Violent threats or actions by a disgruntled current or former employee
- On-the-job incidents
- Sudden death of a senior executive
- Loss of significant business from one or more customers
- Government probes or fines
- Natural disasters
- Boycotts, pickets, or strikes
- A failure in technology
- New competition

Consider this list as a good starting point. It should then be customized for your particular organization. The following is an example of this latter stage:

1. Poor Financial Performance
   a. New competition
   b. Product defects
   c. Underfinanced
2. A Failure in Technology
   a. Product tampering
   b. Security breach
   c. Natural disaster that disrupts a major product or service
   d. Product defects
   e. Distribution breakdown
3. Negative Media Coverage
   a. Malicious rumors
   b. IPO failure
   c. Executive scandal
   d. Poor product report

The company is an Internet startup, www.lit.com, and it specializes in locating first editions of great literature.

Note that the list developed for www.lit.com identifies primary crisis possibilities and then provides an underlying order or structure that allows us to cluster its crises. Although every crisis possesses distinct and unique features, there is always an underlying order and logic that can guide organizations regarding the various types of crises they should prepare for. There is also another reason why clustering crises is so important. A study of crises will reveal that virtually no crisis ever happens in isolation. Before they occur, virtually all crises send out early warning signals. If these signals are picked up and acted upon, then many major crises can be prevented before they occur.

By way of example, let's take the issue of possible employee layoffs or downsizing. Clearly, there are a host of related issues that cluster around this serious potential crisis. For instance, the rumor mill is a major source of misinformation. Negative or incorrect stories in the media can also give credence to this rumor. Simply saying nothing about this possible event may allow employees, customers, and analysts to fill in the blanks. Ultimately, premature employee resignations or early retirements can be an impetus for this possible event to become a reality. The point is that the crisis manager is wise to identify the entire cluster of related disruptions surrounding a major, more obvious crisis.

Also, there is the possibility that a problem will appear in more than one cluster. Identifying such a problem, for example, product defect, is particularly important since it may impact the organization in several different areas, and may denote a primary flaw in the company or an area where the company is highly vulnerable from competitors. See Case 3 for an example of an obvious flaw.

CASE 3: A HOT SIGNAL

McDonald's knew that its coffee was among the hottest—if not the hottest—in the industry. It seemed the fast-food chain also knew its coffee sometimes caused serious injury; however, it didn't consult experts about the issue. Both these issues were seemingly overlooked.

McDonald's reported that the company had received at least 700 complaints of coffee burns ranging from mild to third degree during the last decade. It had settled claims from scalding injuries for more than $500,000.

Therefore, it wasn't surprising when in February 1992, an eighty-one-year-old woman suffered third-degree burns when a cup of McDonald's scalding coffee, placed between her legs, spilled on her groin area. In August 1994, a New Mexico state court jury awarded her $2.9 million in punitive and compensatory damages. The award produced banner headlines nationwide. The judge later reduced that award to $640,000. The woman and McDonald's settled the case for an undisclosed figure.

Public opinion was on McDonald's side: U.S. consumers like their coffee hot—really hot. However, the fast-food chain giant misunderstood the real issue on trial in Albuquerque. The trial wasn't about coffee temperature; it was about corporate concern and responsibility for customers' safety. The multinational giant acted arrogantly and seemed to disregard patrons' safety. Instead of responding quickly and with concern for the customer's health, McDonald's gave the impression that they felt that it was her own fault she got burned.

McDonald's competitors learned a lesson. The Specialty Coffee Association of America put coffee safety on its agenda for its quarterly board meeting. Other companies like Starbucks Coffee Company and Dunkin' Donuts reported publicly that they were evaluating the way they served their coffee and announced that they were providing warnings on their cups. Wendy's temporarily suspended the sale of hot chocolate.

Observation

- Sometimes dealing with minor problems early can prevent catastrophes later on. Even one complaint should be enough (let alone 700) when the safety of a company's product is called into question.

Antecedents

Before assigning a susceptibility score to each potential disruption, it is necessary to identify and assess the internal and external antecedents of organizational crisis. That is, there are a number of known and unknown factors that may affect a crisis. Moreover, we have learned that most crises are not only multiple, but are due to interactions between the technologies of an organization, its structure, human error, the effects of corporate culture, and the attitudes of key executives and managers. In other words, unless one has an understanding of the broader system, actions intended to prevent or respond to one crisis can set off a chain reaction of other crises.

Let's begin by examining some of the key internal antecedents of organization crises.

Executive characteristics. The attitudes and historical behaviors of top management at a particular company often has a direct bearing on how that company manages crises. Certainly some of the worst examples of crisis blunders are the direct results of CEOs who felt that they didn't owe the public an explanation or that they were capable of solving the problem by themselves. There are also top executives who feel they are impervious to crisis. Conversely, there are top executives who understand the need for a crisis management process and are willing to support it with necessary resources. Of course, there are managers somewhere in between these two extremes. Understanding how top management is likely to prepare and respond to crises is critical information for the crisis manager.

Organization demographics. Every organization has a demographic profile that reflects their attitude toward diversity, gender issues, training, hiring practices, and so forth. You might start by simply calculating the size of the organization and the location of employees. How about the skill sets of employees? Gender? Race? Nationality? Age? A company that faces the eminent retirement of most of its top management in the next few years is apt to face a serious replacement crisis. Likewise, a company reluctant to hire minorities faces the possible wrath of many advocacy groups.

Organization history and experience. There are many consumers who will never forgive Exxon. The pictures of those dying oil-covered birds and sea otters are permanent memories. The ability of Johnson & Johnson to correctly handle the Tylenol tampering or McDonald's to immediately bulldoze the California restaurant where several customers were murdered means that these companies have created customer goodwill that will help them in future crises. Airlines have a great deal of experience with catastrophes, such as crashes, and appear to handle them well. However, despite their extensive experience with lost luggage, delayed flights, and angry customers, their success in these areas is quite unimpressive. Think of all the minor crises companies such as L.L. Bean and Lands' End avoid with their "no ask" return policy. Still, there are many businesses that have virtually no experience with moderate or severe crises.

Organization attributes. Every organization has a set of positive and negative attributes, either created by the company or assigned to it by customers, competitors, and others. The Nordstrom department store chain is known for its exceptional service. Enterprise Car Rental is famous for its convenience. Harley-Davidson motorcycles are known for their superior quality and mystique. Children's Hospital Boston is known for its leading edge technology in caring for sick children. And Xerox is famous for its concern for its employees and society. Again, the point is that a company that has a set of positive or negative attributes must realize that these attributes may represent a potential crisis or may effect how the public responds to your crisis. Organizations are advised to conduct the necessary research to correctly identify these attributes. Not only may management be incorrect in attribute assessment, but attributes are constantly changing.

There are also a set of external antecedents that impact the organization. External means that the factors exist outside the organization, and that most often, these factors are beyond the control of the organization.

Competitors. There is little doubt that a competitor can easily turn your small crisis into a catastrophe. Just look at political campaigns.

Still, it is rare that a competitor is that aggressive in the business world. Right! Basic questions to ask yourself are the following:

- Who are your competitors?
- What are your relative strengths and weaknesses compared to your competition?
- How did you respond to their past crisis?
- Are there new competitors entering the market?
- Are there old competitors leaving the market? Why?
- Which potential crises do you share with your competitors?
- Which potential crises are unique to you?

Besides answering these questions, there is a guiding principle that all crisis managers should heed: It is very dangerous to attack a competitor when they are dealing with a crisis.

Suppliers. Suppliers are manufacturers, wholesalers, or other distributors that provide an organization with a finished product, or components that go into a finished product. Often, the inability of a supplier to perform this task can become a very serious crisis. Keebler can't make crackers if their flour supplier is unable to deliver. IBM can't make computers if their components supplier in Malaysia is shut down because of a typhoon. Strikes by truckers and dock workers put organizations out of business. High diesel prices can produce the same results. Companies should avoid being dependent on one or two suppliers, but this is not always possible. It's amazing how many business crises are related to their suppliers.

Consumers and customers. A consumer is a potential customer. This may seem like a small distinction, but in the world of crisis management it is critical. Although the numbers vary, it is far more costly to attract a new customer than to keep an existing customer (perhaps five to eight times more costly). Therefore, it is most appropriate to deal with crises that impact customers before resolving crises that impact consumers. Take care of the people who matter most. Again, this is an area where research is mandatory. What do your customers really care about? Under what conditions will they forgive you or not forgive you? Much of this information can be gathered in conjunction with basic marketing research. A restaurant that mails out thousands of two-for-one coupons may produce a great deal of new traffic but lose long-standing customers because they cannot get into the restaurant.

Regulators. Most organizations must deal with a variety of federal, state, and local regulators. Agencies such as the Food and

Drug Administration, the Federal Communication Commission, and the Occupational Safety and Health Act, literally have the capability of putting you out of business. It is mandatory that every organization, regardless of size, hire qualified lawyers and accountants to monitor and advise. Any organization that serves potentially harmful products to customers will be closely scrutinized. This is a red flag for crisis managers.

Societies. A society represents a group of people, usually defined by geographic borders, shared history, values, and cultural mores. Phrases such as the "Protestant work ethic," "Save for a rainy day," and the "Global community," reflect some of the cultural periods experienced in the American society. Although some would argue that the Internet and other technologies have resulted in a global society, this may be more true for some organizations compared to others. The owner of a local hardware store still defines his society in terms of a neighborhood. A small farming community in Southern Illinois reflects a clearly defined society, feeling very little impact from the outside world. Words like friendship, honesty, and family define their society.

Owners and Boards of Directors. Dominant company owners and authoritative boards are likely to respond to major crises and show little interest in the more minor disruptions. Why? Because they view these more serious crises as possible sources for corporate failure, they tend to focus their resources on the prevention and/or solution of these catastrophic problems. The crisis planner must understand the personalities of owners and board members. In a small business, the crisis planner is likely to be the owner. This certainly may confuse crisis planning.

Employees. The organization's employees are very important in the management of crises. As shown in the Penton Publishing example at the beginning of this chapter, employees can determine whether a company recovers from a major crisis. Motivating employees to invest in the organization and its future leads to better crisis management. Providing a safe work environment, adequate salaries and benefits, and opportunities for advancement may be some of the best crisis prevention tactics. A simple question to ask yourself is, "How do you think your employees would respond when his or her friends are denigrating your organization?" Employee satisfaction and loyalty make crises management much easier.

Combining the various possible crises with an assessment of the relevant antecedent factors provides the susceptibility index. This process is mostly subjective, but there are ways to make it more objective. An example might be to create a susceptibility instrument and distribute it to individuals both inside and outside the organization. Table 3.1 completes the susceptibility index for our imaginary www.lit.com company.

The information contained in Table 3.1 not only provides a general susceptibility index; that is, 5.7 and 5.6, it also indicates the relative strengths and weaknesses in dealing with crises. In our example, organization demographics, new competition, and poor-product reporting represent the more serious areas of susceptibility.

Table 3.1
Crises Susceptibility Index for www.lit.com

Antecedent Variables	Very Negative 1 ------- Very Positive 10
	x score
Executive Characteristics	6.3
Organization Demographics	2.8
Organization History/Experience	4.6
Organization Attributes	4.2
Competitors	6.1
Suppliers	5.7
Consumers/Customers	6.4
Regulators	7.7
Societies	8.5
Owners/Boards	4.3
Employees	6.0
Average Score	5.7

Potential Crises	Susceptibility Index High (1 – 10) Low
➤ Poor financial performance	
• New competition	2.6
• Product defects	7.8
• Under financed	5.3
➤ Failure in technology	
• Product tampering	3.8
• Security breach	6.6
• Natural disasters	3.9
• Product defects	7.5
• Distribution breakdown	4.6
➤ Negative media coverage	
• Malicious rumors	8.3
• IPO failure	5.1
• Executive scandal	7.9
• Poor product report	3.6
Average score	5.6

Create a Probability Index

We can next assign a probability index to each potential crisis. Again, this process is somewhat subjective, based on experience, company history, the experience of similar companies, and so forth. It can be done by individuals both inside and outside the organization. The probability score is also directly influenced by the susceptibility index just discussed. Taking our example to this next level might produce the following results:

Potential Crisis	Probability (0–10.0)
New competition	9.1
Product defects	5.6
Underfinanced	8.3
Product tampering	8.6
Security breach	7.2
Natural disaster	3.6
Distribution breakdown	6.9
Malicious rumors	4.7
IPO failure	7.8
Executive scandal	2.5
Poor product report	6.6

This index suggests that the most likely crises to occur for this company are new competition, product tampering, and being underfinanced. Clearly the strategic plan would differ for each. This leads us to the last phase of the auditing process, completing the classification matrix.

Complete the Classification Matrix

This process, although tedious, provides the crisis manager with a great deal more information upon which to base the crisis plan. Figure 3.4 illustrates how this matrix might look for the www.lit.com organization. Note that there can be more than one crisis in a particular cell, and that each crisis has its assigned susceptibility index and probability index in parentheses.

CONCLUSION

Planning is the bedrock of crisis management. Identifying the vulnerability your company has for crises is a critical first step. It

Figure 3.4
Crisis Classification Matrix for www.lit.com

Threat Level / Response Options	Time Pressure	Intense		Minimal	
	Degree of Control	Low	High	Low	High
Low / Many				Rumors (8.3/4.7)	
Low / Few		Product Tampering (3.8/8.6)	Security Breach (6.6/7.2)	Natural Disaster (3.9/3.6)	Executive Scandal (7.9/2.5)
High / Many		Under-financed (5.3/8.3)	Product Defects (7.8/5.6)	Distribution Breakdown (4.6/6.9)	
High / Few		New Competition (2.6/9.1)		IPO Failure (5.1/7.8)	Poor Product Report (3.6/6.6)

is a warning system that can lead to prevention and minimization when a crisis does occur. Often a crisis is not what it seems. For example, in the aftermath of Hurricane Andrew in 1992, the telephone companies discovered that one of its principal shortages in southern Florida was not poles, wires, or switches but daycare centers. Many of the phone companies' field-operations employees had children and relied on daycare. When the centers were destroyed by the hurricane, someone had to stay home to take care of the children, thereby reducing the workforce at the moment when it was needed the most. The problem was eventually solved by soliciting retirees to attend ad hoc daycare centers, thereby freeing working parents to assist in restoring the telephone network. What could have been a crippling situation ended up being one that kept all types of members of the community involved, and opened up the door to creating goodwill rather than acrimony. Planning, and then executing, is everything.

4

Goal Setting as Part of Crisis Planning

Well done is better than well said.

Benjamin Franklin

Does sex still sell? Take a look at Abercrombie & Fitch's magazine-like catalog, the $6 *A&F Quarterly*. Young women sport little more than $30 T-shirts, and buff guys seem to have a tough time keeping their nether hair tucked into their $60 cargo shorts. And then there are the articles. One in the newest 281-page catalog, sent to 350,000 people, touts Costa Rica as a spring break destination because, among other reasons, prostitution is legal. "Naked News Wire" fills you in on famous people who were photographed in the raw, and tells you how to find out where to go for nude skiing and volleyball.

Now take a look at Abercrombie's stock price, down from $50.75 in April 1999 to a recent $15. What is the reason? The retailer's momentum is off. Sales at stores open at least a year were just 3 percent higher during the fourth quarter of 1999 than in 1998, compared with a 26-percent gain between 1997 and 1998 fourth quarters.

Is the company losing touch with its core audience? Is it going to change its ad strategy? "Absolutely not," snaps Sam N. Shahid, a board member and head of Abercrombie's ad agency. The company is more likely to tweak some of its clothing than put more of it on the models.

It should be noted that Shahid has been courting controversy since the 1980s. As the creative director at Calvin Klein, he drew notice with provocative black-and-white snapshots by Bruce Weber (his collaborator at Abercrombie). In 1992 he left Calvin Klein and landed at the then-fledgling Banana Republic, where he tapped Weber to shoot a campaign to update the retailer's safari image. In one ad, two guys nuzzled. He next opened Shahid & Co., representing (besides Abercrombie) Perry Ellis, Versace, Naturalizer Shoes, and Tse Cashmere.

Based on the history of Sam Shahid, top management at Abercrombie knew they were probably taking a risk in giving him free rein with their advertising. Perhaps his creative, hip advertising style was viewed as very appealing to their customer base. Maybe they did no or very little background research. Or perhaps they misinterpreted the results.

All would agree that Abercrombie is experiencing a serious crisis. By the time you read this book, they may no longer exist. Do they have a crisis plan? It appears unlikely since the response by Shahid can be interpreted as unyielding. Should they have a crisis plan? Absolutely.

What should be the objectives of the crisis plan? That is, what should the crisis plan accomplish? Like any set of business objectives, they should (1) be based on the strength, weakness, opportunity, and threat (S.W.O.T.) analysis; (2) identify the target market; and (3) be followed by strategies that delineate how the objectives will be achieved. The purpose of this chapter is to identify the process of establishing objectives as part of crisis planning.

Undoubtedly, a critical part of every planning process is the establishment of relevant goals and objectives. Once the company has performed a S.W.O.T. analysis, it can proceed to develop specific goals for the planning period. This stage of the process is called goal formulation. Managers use the term "goals" to describe objectives that are specific with respect to magnitude and time. Turning objectives into measurable goals facilitates management planning, implementation, and control. There are also specific characteristics associated with goal formation.

MULTIPLE GOALS

Very few businesses pursue only one objective. Most businesses pursue a mix of objectives including profitability, sales growth, market-share improvement, risk containment, innovativeness, and reputation. Note that the last three in the list appear to link to potential crises, either as antecedent or result. As will be discussed later in this chapter, these goals may suggest other goals that are even more closely tied to crisis management.

HIERARCHY OF GOALS

No business function, including crisis management, can operate independently. To be effective, the planning process must operate within a hierarchy of goals. At the top are corporate goals, which should reflect the interests of the firm's major stakeholders, especially stockholders. This level in the hierarchy generally defines the product or market scope of the business and establishes key targets for the corporation as a whole. Corporate policy goals need to be translated into specific, measurable criteria. In the United States, stock price and earnings per share (and their growth rates) occupy the highest position in the hierarchy with return on assets or investments (ROA or ROI) close behind. Because financial markets and corporate raiders typically pay close attention to these measures, top management understandably tends to give them very high priority. In Japan, adequate returns, building market share, and providing premium products are more likely to be paramount goals.

Within the hierarchy of corporate goals, each function is given specific goals it must accomplish. Marketing, for example, is usually responsible for sales revenue, market share, and operating profit. Thus, marketing strategies are formulated to achieve specific sales, share, and profit objectives. In many leading companies, marketing is responsible not only for absolute profits (in dollars) but also for achieving target ROA and ROI results.

If the best strategy we can come up with exceeds the goals we initially established, we should adjust the goals upwards. Conversely, if we are unable to come up with a strategy that is likely to achieve the preestablished goals, we should lower those goals (or perhaps we should be replaced by a manager who can create strategies that will achieve the goals). It is far better to admit the probable outcomes of a particular business program early than to permit an organization to operate under false delusions that put it on a course with failure. There is a delicate balance between setting goals that inspire an organization and proposing unrealistic goals that cause managers to write plans they know are meaningless. When unrealistic goals are set, the whole strategic planning process becomes merely a game. Effective goal setting causes an organization to stretch to achieve its full capacity, but is realistic enough to generate commitment on the part of its managers. There are other criteria that effective goals should meet.

Good Goals

Setting goals remains one of the most misunderstood aspects of business planning. Partly this is a result of the assumption by many that developing business goals is equivalent to developing personal goals. In fact, there are guidelines for business goal generation.

The first criteria relates to our previous discussion. Goals and objectives must be arranged hierarchically, from the most to the least important. This perspective differs somewhat from our earlier discussion of hierarchy. This assumes that hierarchy follows the structure of the organization from top to bottom, assumes that goals at the corporate level are more important than those at the functional level, and that functional goals are more important than goals at the operative level, and, so forth. Rather than using the organization hierarchy as a surrogate for importance, goals can be ordered by employing other evaluative criteria. Time, cost, urgency, and competitive response may prove useful criteria. Often the ranking refers to a contingency situation. That is, "I can't increase sales until I access an additional number of outlets for my product, and I can't accomplish this until I am able to reduce the cost charged to the outlets."

The second criteria is that the goal must be stated clearly. One way to make a goal statement clear is to quantify as many elements of the statement as possible. Moreover, the terminology and numbers should have a common understanding to all relevant parties. Financial and accounting goals can contain a myriad of technical terms and ratios that are neither understood or appreciated by those outside the discipline.

Another factor to consider in making a goal statement more clear is to make certain that each goal statement contains only one primary element. For example, to present the following goal statement is quite confusing because it contains two elements: "to increase market share by 5% and profitability by 10%." Finally, goal statements can be tested for their clarity. Have a sample of relevant experts read your goal statements and have them report on the clarity of each.

A third criteria to apply to the development of your goal statement is that each goal must be realistic. While it is good for a stated goal to make you stretch as an organization, it is also demoralizing and wasteful to strive to reach a goal that is unrealistic. The S.W.O.T. analysis should serve as the primary reference point to gauge the achievability of a goal. For example, having patent or copyright protection may allow a company to maintain a distinct competitive advantage and strive for higher market-share objectives than a competitor who does not have these benefits. Likewise, lack of cash or access to a line of credit may restrict any kind of growth-related objectives. Of course, unrealistic goals could just as easily be set too low. Low-balling your goal statements may mean you always reach your goal but never reach your true potential. Again, the S.W.O.T. results should be your touchstone.

All goals must be consistent. This becomes more difficult as an organization gets larger or goes global. One might think that a company such as AT&T or Federated Stores has a "goal master" who constantly monitors company goals from top to bottom, but they don't. Goals that are not in sync or even contradict are common in businesses of all sizes. In fact, such contradictions may often be the source of crisis. Consequently, this criteria will be revisited later in this chapter when we discuss specific goals for crisis planning.

Finally, all goals should have an appropriate time frame. Involved individuals must have a reasonable deadline for achieving the targeted goals. For example, a manager may urge her assistant to broaden her education and skills by taking college courses. In spite of regular encouragement, the employee may not take the course unless the two agree on some time frame, say "in the next year I will take two college courses."

A final warning should be noted. Ideally, all goals should be measurable. However, not all goals can be measured precisely, a factor that limits the applicability of goal setting. For instance, consulting firms face the challenge of trying to satisfy their clients' needs. Consultants have to be creative because each client seeks solutions to novel problems.

Trying to set measurable goals for jobs that do not have measurable outcomes is often counterproductive because the goals rarely relate directly to the outcome. In the consulting example, the only goal is client satisfaction, which is a subjective outcome and tough to measure. The firm will not be served well by giving its consultants efficiency goals that are not related to this desired outcome.

THE ROLE OF THE MISSION STATEMENT
IN GOAL SETTING

An organization exists to accomplish something: to make cars, lend money, provide a night's lodging, and so on. It's specific mission or purpose is usually clear when the business starts. Over time the mission may lose its relevance because of changed business conditions or may become unclear as the corporation adds new products or markets to new customers.

When management senses that the organization is drifting from its mission, it must renew its search for purpose. According to Peter Drucker, it is time to ask some fundamental questions:

- What is your business?
- Who is the customer?
- What is value to the customer?
- What will our business be?
- What should our business be?

These simple-sounding questions are among the most difficult the company will ever have to answer. Nevertheless, successful companies continuously raise these questions and answer them thoughtfully and thoroughly.

Organizations develop mission statements to share with managers, employees, outside stakeholders, and (in many cases) customers. A well-developed mission statement provides employees with a shared sense of purpose, direction, and opportunity. The statement guides geographically dispersed employees to work independently and yet collectively toward realizing the organization's goals. Mission statements are at their best when they are guided by a vision, an almost impossible dream that will provide direction for the company for the next ten to twenty years. Sony's former president, Akio Morita, wanted everyone to have access to "personal portable sound," so his company created the Walkman and portable CD player.

Here is an example of Motorola's mission statement: "The purpose of Motorola is to honorably serve the needs of the community by providing products and services of superior quality at a fair price to our customers; to do this so as to earn as adequate profit which is required for the total enterprise to grow; and by so doing provide the opportunity for our employees and shareholders to achieve their reasonable personal objectives."

Good mission statements have three major characteristics. First, they focus on a limited number of goals. The statement "We want to produce the highest quality products, offer the most service, achieve the widest distribution, and sell at the lowest prices" claims too much. Second, mission statements stress the major policies and values that the company wants to honor. Policies define how the company will deal with stakeholders, employees, customers, suppliers, distributors, and other important groups. Policies narrow the range of individual discretion so that employees act consistently on important issues. Third, they define the major competitive scopes within which the company will operate:

- Industry scope—the range of industries in which a company will operate
- Products and application scope—the range of products and applications that a company will supply
- Competence scope—the range of technological and other core competencies that a company will master and leverage
- Market-segment scope—the type of market or customers a company will serve
- Virtual scope—the number of channel levels from raw material to final product and distribution in which a company will participate
- Geographical scope—the range of regions, countries, or country groups in which a company will operate

Mission statements should not be revised every few years in response to every new turn in the economy. However, a company must redefine its mission if that mission has lost its credibility or no longer defines an optimal course for the company. Kodak has redefined itself from a film company to an image company so that it could add digital imaging. IBM has redefined itself from a hardware and software manufacturer to a "builder of networks." Sara Lee is redefining itself by outsourcing manufacturing and becoming a marketer of brands.

Ultimately, the mission statement establishes a general direction for the entire organization, the objectives that lead it. Mission statements that are confusing or misleading can often be the source of crises. "Serving society" sounds grand and altruistic but places a tremendous burden on a company that is dominated by its stockholders and their needs and wants. Likewise a company that espouses words like "quality" or "service" takes the risk that stakeholders will misinterpret.

Ultimately the company's mission can be turned into detailed supporting objectives for each level of management. Each manager will have objectives and be responsible for reaching them.

As an illustration, the International Minerals and Chemical Corporation is in many businesses, including the fertilizer business. The fertilizer division does not say that its mission is to produce fertilizer. Instead, it says that its mission is to "increase agricultural productivity." This mission leads to a hierarchy of objectives: business objectives, marketing objectives, and, finally, a marketing strategy. The mission of increasing agricultural productivity leads to the company's business objective of researching new fertilizers that promise higher yields. But research is expensive and requires improved profits to plow back into research programs. So a major objective becomes to improve profits. Profits can be improved by increasing sales or reducing costs. Sales can be increased by enlarging the company's share of the U.S. market and by entering new foreign markets.

SETTING GOALS FOR THE CRISIS PLAN

Having provided an overview of the goal development process, it is now appropriate to discuss how goals are created as part of crisis planning. Because you have chosen to engage in comprehensive crises planning, we can assume that one overriding goal is in place—the crisis will be dealt with proactively rather than reactively. In addition, goal formulation differs somewhat in crisis planning because of the following characteristics:

- There is a need to think both proactively and reactively about goals
- Goals must be considered in light of how they will impact the entire organization
- Goal development must begin with top management
- Goals must reflect the corporate needs and values

We have already discussed the benefits of taking a proactive rather than a reactive position toward crisis management. Still, there are crises that will get through the cracks, and a reactive response is necessary. Therefore, goals relative to crisis should probably be categorized into two categories, proactive and reactive. Examples of the former might include the following: "decrease customer complaints by 40 percent during the next six months," or "increase employee training opportunities by 50 percent in the next year." Examples of reactive goals might look as follows: "All employee injuries must be reported to the vice president of human resources within twenty-four hours after treatment," or "No stories are to be released to the media until they are approved by the crisis management committee."

Clearly, crisis-related goals do not just affect the entity involved. The causes of most crisis are not only multiple, but are due to interactions between the technologies of an organization, its structure, human errors, the effects of corporate culture, and the attitudes of key executives and managers. A recent incident with Sears illustrates this point. Because of falling revenues, Sears decided to introduce a bonus plan designed to bring more business into its auto repair facilities. Unfortunately, dishonest workers and managers collected even larger bonuses by charging customers for parts not installed and services not performed. Thus, the attempt to solve one crisis created an even larger crisis by seriously denigrating the reputation of Sears. And, not just the Sears' Automotive departments, but all the departments.

Although it is always important for top management to support corporate goals, it is even more important with crisis-related goals. Why? Primarily because this whole notion of managing crisis is a recent phenomenon, it needs a champion at the highest level possible. Moreover, if you have top executives who believe silence is the best method to protect the company's reputation or appease unhappy customers and employees, than that philosophy should be reflected in the stated goals. Similarly, the order in which these goals are placed should be dictated by top management.

All these factors come together under the heading of "corporate philosophy" or "value system." Such philosophies set the general tone as to how the organization will deal with crises, both serious and minor. Companies such as Hewlett-Packard, 3M, and Motorola are well-known for their corporate values that stimulate innovation and new product development, but do all this with the highest standards possible. It often comes down to ethics—personal and professional—and to integrity. Case 4 illustrates how one business suffered from a lack of goals.

CASE 4: DELI IN THE LURCH

David and Sally Foster opened Deli-on-the-Green in April 1972. Originally from Philadelphia, they fell in love with Winston-Salem, North Carolina in the fall of 1971 when they drove David Jr. to begin his freshman year at Wake Forest University. The moderate climate, the beautiful scenery, and access to a dynamic student body quickly convinced them that moving Dave's Deli to North Carolina was the thing to do.

Finding a recently vacated store with 2,700 square feet of usable space one block from campus and across the street from one of the prettiest parks in the city clinched the deal. And for twenty-five years the decision seemed well-founded and in fact, it was. The deli was very popular and quickly became a destination for Wake Forest University students, especially those on that side of campus. Then in the fall of 1996 things began to fall apart.

First, it was little things. The meat supplier they had used for twelve years went out of business, and they were forced to use a supplier in Atlanta, who charged 30 percent more. Next, the city decided to widen the street in front of the store, taking nearly three feet of valuable frontage. More important, for almost five months, barricades and machinery made access to the deli almost impossible. Then the major catastrophe happened. Due to a malfunction in the refrigerator, a container of mayonnaise became tainted and eleven customers suffered from botulism. Although David's liability insurance took care of the medical bills, law suits, and so forth, the harm to the reputation of the business was severe. Six months later Dave sold out to a health food chain.

Observation

Where these events out of Dave's control or could they have been anticipated, or even prevented, if he had crisis-related goals in place?

A FEW WORDS ON BUDGETING

One of the mysteries of running a business is calculating the budget. Whether it is determined by the chief financial officer, the owner of the business, or the situation at hand, no one is sure whether we are underspending, overspending, or right on target. In an ideal business plan, the determination of the budget should follow immediately following the delineation of objectives and goals. Thus, we feel obligated to follow this pattern as well. An overview of budgeting is followed by a discussion of how money should be allocated to crisis planning.

An Overview of Budgeting

Despite the fact that billions of dollars are spent on business expenses every year, the majority of the companies spending these dollars use decision processes that are based on little, if any, strategic thinking. Although this pattern has not proven detrimental to many of these companies, there is growing evidence that managers are using more sophisticated techniques in setting appropriations and budgets. Traditional subjective methods are gradually being replaced by data-driven approaches. These approaches may provide an additional competitive advantage to those willing to commit to them. First, however, we will discuss the subjective methods of appropriation.

Percentage of Sales

The percentage-of-sales technique is probably the most popular of the budgetary methods. Management bases the appropriation on a fixed percentage of sales of the previous year, of an anticipated year, or of an average of several years. To illustrate, if sales were $3 million on average for the last three years, management using this technique might pick 5 percent of that average and allocate $150,000. One advantage of this method is that expenditures are directly related to funds available—the more the company sold last year, the more it presumably has available for this year. Another advantage is its simplicity. If business people know last year's sales and have decided what percentage they wish to spend, the calculation is easy.

The percentage-of-sales method suffers from several serious limitations, however. Most notably, it assumes that marketing is a result of sales rather than a cause of sales. It does not take into account the possibility that sales may decline because of underspending on marketing. Also, this method does not include the possibility of diminishing returns(meaning that after a certain point additional dollars may generate fewer and fewer sales. In short, using the percentage of sales may mean underspending when the sales opportunities are high and overspending when the potential is low.

Perhaps the most effective manner in which to use the percentage-of-sales technique is to examine both past sales and forecasted sales. This examination also assures that market potential is accounted for when the forecast is considered. Regardless of its limitations, the percentage-of-sales method will no doubt remain popular.

Unit of Sales

The unit-of-sales method is very much like the percentage-of-sales technique. Instead of dollar sales, though, the base is the physical volume of either past or future sales. Toyota, for example, would base their appropriation for Camry on the 38,000 units they expect to sell in the United States next year rather than the value of those 38,000 units. This unit value is then multiplied by a fixed amount of money (for example, $125) to derive a total appropriation of $4,750,000. This method exhibits the same strengths and weakness as the percentage-of-sales method, and the same solutions apply. It is commonly used for high-ticket items such as automobiles and appliances.

Competitive Parity

Many businesses base their allocations on competitors' expenditures. Information on expenditures is available readily through sources such as Advertising Age, A. C. Nielsen, and government reports. This technique is rarely the sole determinant of the appropriation.

The competitive parity technique has three advantages. First, it recognizes the importance of competition. Second, it often helps minimize battles between competitors. Because competitors are all spending about the same, they tend not to try to outspend one another. Finally, this approach is simple to use because the only information required is the dollar amount expended by competitors.

The fact that this technique is based on a simple dollar amount also suggests limitation. Important competitors may vary widely in the size and direction for their budgets, so comparisons may be hard to make. Another drawback is that competitive parity assumes that a company's objectives are the same as its competitors, and this can be a treacherous assumption. It also assumes that competitors' allocations are correct. Finally, information on competitive expenditures is available only after the money has been spent, so it may not indicate future selling.

All You Can Afford

With the all-you-can-afford method, the amount left over after all the other relevant company expenditures are made is allocated. Companies of all types and sizes use this method. It is particularly popular when introducing a new product. As unsophisticated as the approach appears, it often produces effective results.

In contrast to the predetermined budgeting methods that are based on simple rules of thumb and industry traditions, several budgeting techniques are based on the strategy itself. These bottom-up approaches begin with the input of people implementing the strategy, continue on to the various managers, and ultimately reach top management, accompanied with documentation supporting the budget amount requested. Admittedly, these techniques are more difficult to use but insure that the marketing communication plan will be implemented effectively. We explore four strategy-based budgetary methods: the objective-task, mathematical model, experimental, and payout planning methods.

Objective Task

The most popular strategic technique is the objective-task method. With this method, the manager first studies the market. Then the manager defines specific objectives for a particular time period. After setting the objectives, the manager determines how much money will be necessary to achieve them. If the associated costs are greater than the money available, then either the objectives are adjusted or more funds are found.

The main advantage of this method is that it develops the budget from the ground up, so that objectives are implemented strategically. It does not rely on factors outside the control of the decision maker, such as past sales or competitors' spending. The second advantage is that the task method works well for new product launches such as the RAV4. In these change situations, historical and competitive information do not provide useful budgeting guidelines. The objective-task method has one key drawback: Its results are only as good as the stated objectives and the accuracy of the dollar amounts assigned to each objective. Setting objectives and assigning accurate dollar amounts are difficult tasks.

Mathematical Models

During the last several decades, the use of quantitative techniques in budgeting has grown but has not found wide acceptance. These quantitative methods may apply mathematical models from other fields, such as physics or psychology, or may use models developed specifically for business.

Mathematical models have not been widely accepted for a variety of reasons. First, they require experimental and formal analysis techniques beyond the capabilities of many companies. Second, the process is time consuming and expensive. Third, models from other fields have not been successfully modified to apply to business, and little agreement exists as to the reliability of these budgeting models. Although new quantitative budgeting models are being proposed, their extensive use in actual practice will probably be slow in coming.

The Experimental Approach

The experimental approach is an alternative to modeling. The manager uses tests and experiments for different budget options in one or more market areas and uses the results to guide budget decisions. Before, during, and after the expenditure, sales and awareness would be measured in each market. By comparing the results, managers can estimate how the varying budget levels might perform nationwide. The budget that produced the best results would then be used.

To a great extent, this technique eliminates the problems associated with the other budgetary approaches. The major drawbacks of this approach are the time and expense (in the low six figures annually) involved in getting the data and the difficulty of controlling the environment. Dow Chemical Company has used the experimentation approach for many years. The company has increased total sales and profits while decreasing advertising costs.

Payout Planning

The payout plan is often used with other budget-setting methods to assess the investment value of the tasks being funded. It projects future revenues generated and costs incurred, usually for a two- or three-year period. Its purpose is to show what level of expenditures needs to be made, what level of return might be expected, and what time period is necessary before the return will occur. Payout planning is a useful budgetary technique when a new product is introduced with a commitment to invest heavily in marketing to stimulate awareness and product acceptance. It acknowledges the likelihood that this situation will diminish company profits for the first year or two. Management naturally wants estimates of both the length of time that marketing dollars must be invested before sales occur and the expected profit flow once the brand has become established.

The payout plan is a useful planning tool, but it has limitations. Most notably, it cannot account for all the uncontrollable factors that may affect the plan. New competitors, legislation, natural disasters, and new technologies are just a few of the contingencies influencing the plan.

Assessing the Situation

In deciding the amount of money to allocate, the astute decision maker should evaluate the key situation factors. Businesses consider the following six factors when determining the appropriation:

- The product, including its type, stage in the life cycle, and strategic components
- The market
- The competition
- The financial condition of the company
- Research guidelines
- The distribution system

The Product

Certain product elements have a tremendous impact on the appropriation. For instance, it takes a larger amount of money to launch a new product than to keep an old one. The same is true for convenience products compared with durable products. Consumer durables, such as furniture and appliances, require an emphasis on personal selling because sales representatives can differentiate the products for consumers, tailor the presentation to meet the prospects' needs, and use persuasive tactics to convince buyers to make such a high-cost purchase. Also, emotion-based products such as cosmetics, perfumes, and cars profit more from advertising than do products bought for primarily rational reasons, such as industrial machinery.

The Market

Both the size and nature of the market influence the appropriation. Manufacturers who expect to cover a national market rather than a regional one will obviously spend more money. Maxwell House Coffee directs all its marketing efforts at coffee drinkers, whereas Gallo Winery tries to turn nonwine drinkers into wine drinkers. These opposite strategies require different tactics and different dollar requirements to support them. Characteristics of the market, including demographics and psychographics, the attitudes and perceptions of the consumer toward the manufacturer, the amount of brand loyalty toward the firm and its competitors, and the amount of product use should also be considered in the appropriation process.

The Competition

Many companies monitor the expenditure of their competition and match these amounts either directly or proportionately. Expenditure information is available through observation or industry statistics. Matching is usually an ineffective strategy. There are instances, however, when a major competitor dramatically increases the budget for a particular brand, and the only recourse is to match this increase.

The Company's Financial Condition

When a company faces falling profits or during a general economic downturn, marketing communication budgets, especially advertising and public relations, are often cut first in firms that view marketing communication as a cost, not an investment. Then, when business booms, expenditures are usually reinstated. This strategy can backfire. Firms that continue their spending during poor economic conditions do better in the long run than firms that decrease or eliminate such spending.

Realistically, however, the allocation is limited by what a company can afford. As a practical matter, a ceiling on the allocation always exists. The manager should be aware of this approximate dollar limit before beginning the planning process.

Research Guidelines

Some companies, such as small companies in furniture manufacturing fields, use little research to guide their decisions; they rely instead on experience and tradition. For the more sophisticated organization, marketing surveys, media data, census material, forecasts, and many other types of research are available.

The Distribution System

A channel of distribution can be quite long and include many intermediaries (that is, wholesalers and retailers). Or it can be quite short and direct, as it is for a manufacturer who uses a catalog and the mail to distribute products. A long, complex channel may require a large appropriation to support the product because of the divided efforts of the intermediaries. For example, Coca-Cola Company Inc. follows an intensive distribution policy because its products must be available in every possible outlet. Because these outlets usually carry competing brands of soft drinks as well, Coca-Cola cannot expect the intermediaries to carry much of the marketing communication effort. A retailer may engage in some cooperative advertising, but little more. Consequently, Coca-Cola must make use of extensive mass marketing communication, especially advertising and couponing that will pull the product through the channel.

In contrast, clothing manufacturer Hart, Schaffner, and Marx distributes its suits through an exclusive dealership arrangement. Because the retailers are guaranteed the sole right to sell the brand, they in turn provide certain efforts for the manufacturer. The retailer will engage in extensive personal selling as well as local advertising. Much of the marketing effort and cost, then, is taken off the shoulders of the manufacturer.

BUDGETING FOR CRISIS MANAGEMENT

All the techniques and situations discussed may have applications to crisis management budgeting. In this case, however, there should be an assessment of the crisis matrix introduced in Chapter 3, along with the prescribed probability index. Again, one should always be cognizant that both of these activities must be customized for each business. For example, an airline might appropriate $10 million to crisis management for crash possibilities. Similarly, a local restaurant might appropriate $7,000 to liability insurance. Despite the huge difference when making a direct comparison, the dollar amount for each company is significant. More will be said about budgeting for crisis management in Chapter 5.

CONCLUSION

Without a clear delineation of goals the organization is likely to spread resources too thinly and lack focus for its activities. Managers who are unable or unwilling to set meaningful goals will find it difficult to work out effective plans. Care needs to be taken when defining goals so that they are specific and measurable. At the same time possible consequences and side effects must be taken into account. Planning is an integrated process and the establishment of goals at one level will generally affect goals at the other levels in the organization. Goal formulation becomes even more complicated in crisis situations.

Once goals are determined, the budgeting process follows. Budgeting may be conducted using a variety of techniques—both subjective and objective. There are also situational factors to consider. Ultimately, crisis management will not be successful unless it is included in the budgetary process.

5

Organizing to Manage Crisis

There is great audacity in the willingness to change, and more
than a little optimism.

Robert Crais

REDESIGNING ALCOA

Paul H. O'Neill became the chairman of the Aluminum Company
of America in 1991, "becoming the first outsider in the company's
103-year history to call the shots. Although O'Neill knew precious
little about the aluminum game, he quickly refocused Alcoa on its
notoriously cyclical aluminum businesses, while reassuring investors that there would be no more wild earnings gyrations on his
watch. Critics figured that O'Neill was in for a few unpleasant sur-
prises. But Alcoa's return on equity has averaged 15% since he arrived on the scene, 50% above the average of the previous decade."

O'Neill has initiated major changes in the organization. On September 2, 1991, he began "a massive overhaul of management meant
to refashion Alcoa into a highly decentralized outfit." At a management powwow in Pittsburgh some fifty worldwide senior executives
were stunned to learn that O'Neill planned to give Alcoa's twenty-

five business-unit managers unprecedented leeway to run their businesses. Also, two levels of top management would be wiped out. Says Australian business-unit manager Robert F. Slagle, one of the fortunate twenty-five: "We felt liberated."

O'Neill chose to eliminate Alcoa's hierarchical chain of command. "Frontline managers will get plenty of decision-making authority— but also the accountability that goes with it. O'Neill expects all of Alcoa's various business lines—it makes everything from aluminum sheet for beverage cans to aerospace parts—to score significant gains over their rivals within two years."

O'Neill also initiated additional changes. "To extend Alcoa's reach in the faster-growing European and Asian markets, he set up joint ventures with foreign partners. And to smooth out Alcoa's earnings performance, O'Neill and his team negotiated longer-term metals contracts. They also have set up an innovative variable-rate dividend plan to reward investors who stay with the company during economic downturns.

These changes pose unusual challenges. "O'Neill's gambit, inspired by his own often-unconventional thinking about management, is hardly risk-free. He's counting on untested line executives to muster the managerial skill and know-how to quickly ratchet up quality and efficiency to world standards. And he's pouring on the demands at a time when aluminum prices are at a five-year low, after plunging over 30% this past year," said Slagle.

A cursory review of books and cases on crisis management consistently advise that some level of reorganization is necessary for crisis management to prove effective. Normally, the greater the catastrophic possibility faced by a business, the larger and more inclusive the reorganization. Thus, Delta Airlines has a crisis management committee, comprised of individuals working in all the company's major functions, and a total size ranging between fifty and sixty people. The objective of this committee is primarily to engage in long-range planning; initiating action when a crash or near crash occurs. Another group deals with actual crisis response.

Although this approach to organizing for crisis has proven effective, it does not fully reflect the approach proposed in this book. Rather than thinking about organizing for crisis as primarily a structural decision, we advocate reorganizing for crisis as a contingency approach, dependent upon the specific elements considered important in a particular business.

This chapter begins with an overview of the principles associated with sound organizational design and redesign. This discussion serves as a foundation for the crisis-specific discussion that follows.

BASIC CONSIDERATIONS
OF ORGANZATIONAL DESIGN

One of the purposes of management is to enable people to work effectively toward accomplishing organizational goals. To do this, a structure of roles must be designed and maintained by management. To make the role fully operational, the individual should have a clear concept of the major activities or duties involved, a clear understanding of the relationships of that role with others where coordination is needed, and the needed information to carry out the duties. However, these principles are not iron-clad rules, but rather the foundation for understanding how organizing processes affect the behaviors of individuals within the firm.

Bases of Departmentation

Departmentation is the grouping of activities in organization structures. There are four basic forms of departmentation that have proved useful: function, place, product, and customer. Regardless of the type of organizing processes used, each process makes it possible for the organization to group its members with respect to certain basic activities.

Departmentation by Function

Functional grouping of activities is a widely used and accepted managerial practice. It covers what organizations actually do, namely, production, marketing, and financing. Sometimes the basic functions do not really appear on an organization chart, however. For example, hospitals have no marketing departments, and churches have no production departments. Rather, these functions are given other names. Thus, for example, airlines (TWA, KLM, and Allegheny) use the terms operations (production), traffic, and finance; large department stores (Lazarus, May Company, JC Penny, and Sears) use the terms finance, general merchandising, publicity, and general superintendent. In the latter case, the traditional functions of production, selling, and finance have been combined with other activities.

Departmentation by Place

Departmentation based on geographic area is a rather common method for organizing physically dispersed firms. The principle is that all activities in a given territory should be grouped and assigned to one manager, on the assumption that efficiency will improve. Place departmentation is used by the major airline companies. In United Airlines' organization chart, the territories of the three major areas are further subdivided into nine districts. Other examples of place deparmentation are large police departments that divide the city into precincts and department stores that assign floor walkers, janitors, and window washers to various parts of the store. Similarly, many governmental agencies, such as the Internal Revenue Service, the Federal Reserve Board, the federal courts, and the Postal Service, adopt place deparmentation as the basis of organization in their efforts to provide nationwide services. Many multinational firms use this basis of departmentation because of the differences in cultural and legal factors operating in each country. The lack of uniformity in market structures, differences in production methods, and divergent patterns of national traditions and norms make geographical considerations important for the firm's success.

Departmentation by Product

The grouping of activities on the basis of product has been an emerging trend in large multiproduct companies such as GM, Ford, Procter & Gamble, General Foods, Corning Glass Works, and Mack Trucks. Typically, these organizations once had a functional basis of departmentation, but their growth and subsequent managerial problems made functional departmentation uneconomical and led to a reorganization on the basis of product.

This strategy permits top management to delegate extensive authority to a product-line manager over the manufacturing, sales, service, and engineering functions that relate to a given product or product line. General Motors' organization chart reflects this as one of the corporation's bases for departmentation. Each division— Chevrolet, Buick, Pontiac, and so on—has considerable operating autonomy, with its own manufacturing plants, sales force, distribution centers, and research and development staffs. Product managers are given a considerable degree of profit responsibility by top management for their specific product lines.

Departmentation by Customer

The grouping of activities to reflect the interests of different customers is commonly found in business firms. Customers are the key to the way many utilities are organized, because the various customers make varied demands on the utilities services. Customers are the key to the way activities are grouped, and the heads of all groups report to one manager.

Concepts of Coordination

It has often been said that good people can make any organization effective. It has also been found that ambiguity in an organization is a good thing in that it forces teamwork, since people know that they must work together and cooperate to get anything done. Teamwork is especially relevant in team sports; although coaches may spend hours practicing against foreign teams, the actual game situation is one of ambiguity for both offensive and defensive players. However, during practice sessions, coaches develop players who want to cooperate and work together most effectively. To do this, players need to know the part they are to play in any cooperative effort and how each player relates to the others. Coordination is required to design and maintain these systems of roles.

Unity of Command

According to traditional-management theorists, such as Taylor, Fayol, and Weber, one manager should be in charge of an area of responsibility. Moreover, a chain of command should be established so that all organization members know to whom they report and who reports to them. No confusion should exist among the individuals responsible for organizational activities over who gives orders and who implements them. The unity-of-command principle forms the basis for the hierarchy found in most organizations.

The scalar principle refers to the chain of direct authority relationships from manager to subordinate throughout the organization. The basis idea of this principle is that every employee should know his or her area of responsibility in the organization and that no one individual should report to more than one superior. If this principle is followed, subordinates know who delegates authority to them and to whom matters beyond their authority must be referred.

Span of Control

Span of control deals with the number of subordinates who report directly to a superior. The problem of span of control is as old as organizations. The problem arises from the belief that a manager's mind is not complex enough to supervise too many people. This belief has been fostered by military organizations' finding that narrow spans of control were most effective in combat situations.

Traditional-management practitioners also specified that the number of subordinates reporting to any one manager should range between four and twelve.

In actual experience, one finds a variety of practices. In a survey of 100 large companies, the American Management Association found that the number of executives reporting to the president varied from one to twenty-four; only twenty-six presidents had six or fewer subordinates, and the median number was nine. Comparable results have been found by other researchers. One consistent result is that in large organizations (those with at least $1 billion sales), the span of control at the top tends to be no more than twelve, with the span decreasing as company size decreases.

In summary, some confusion has arisen from specific statements about the ideal maximum number of subordinates who should report to any one supervisor. There is, of course, no one such number. Rather, the maximum number of subordinates a manager can effectively manage is a function of several contingency factors, as well as several behavioral consequences. Although there is probably a magical limit, that number will vary in accordance with the contingency factors and the importance attributed to them by the manager and the organization.

Authority Structure

The underlying thread that makes the division of work and its coordination possible is the authority structure of the firm. The authority structure is the means by which activities can be placed in a manager's job and the coordination of the organization's activities carried out. Thus authority is the manager's tool for exercising considerable discretion in creating an environment conducive to individual performance. Authority is the cement of the organization's structure.

Authority provides for the direction and control of the flow of decisions from the top of the organization downward through the unity of command. "Authority" is the term for the rights needed to carry out one's organizational obligations. Executive authority includes, therefore, the rights of decision and command with respect to the organizational activities of one's subordinates. For example, if A tells B to perform a task, B may not perform it. But if B does, there are two possible reasons. First, A may have convinced B by providing certain information that has led B to perform the task. Second, B may have accepted A's decision without really giving the decision any thought, feeling that it was A's right to do so. This second instance is an example of Weber's legitimate authority. Traditional-management theorists maintained that authority always comes from top management and is legitimized by the person in that role.

Responsibility

Responsibility may be thought of as an owed obligation, one acquired when an individual accepts an assignment of certain objectives, activities, and duties. The manager has duties to carry out and is responsible for the actions of his or her subordinates. Since authority is the discretionary right to carry out assignments and responsibility is the obligation to accomplish the task it follows that authority should correspond to responsibility. Responsibility for actions can be neither greater nor less than authority. For example, there are real limits to the decision a foreman can or should make and to the authority and responsibility he or she should have. A production foreman has no authority to change a salesperson's compensation; a regional sales manager has no authority in somebody else's region. A production foreman usually lacks the competence and the knowledge to work out adequate pay plans for salespeople.

Accountability

Organizational authority is the degree of discretion conferred on people to make it possible for them to use their judgment. If a subordinate accepts the manager's decision and it falls within his or her zone of indifference, the manager can hold the subordinate accountable. Accountability is the subordinate's acceptance of a given task to perform because she or he is a member in the organization. Accountability also requires each member of the organization to report on his or her discharge of responsibilities and to be judged fairly on the basis of his or her record of accomplishment. In the case of the secretary and manager, the secretary is accountable to the manager for dictation. Thus accountability, unlike authority and responsibility, always flows from the bottom up. It is an explicit contract to perform certain task-related activities in return for some reward, usually money.

Oftentimes authority and responsibility are misused. For example, a college book salesperson that is given authority to work a given geographical territory cannot be held responsible for making faculty members choose certain books. However, the sales manager has the authority to use certain resources to obtain sales where possible. In this case, the proper balance between authority and responsibility is reached when the sales manager manages his or her territory in the best way possible.

Delegation of Authority

Most failures in effective delegation occur not because of the manager's lack of understanding of the principles of delegation, but because of unwillingness to apply them in practice. Three basic personal attitudes affect the delegation of authority. First, a manager must be willing to give another person a chance. Decision making always involves some discretion for the decision maker, and this means that a subordinate's decision might differ from the one the supervisor would have made. Second, the manager must be willing to give subordinates the right to make decisions. One reason for Ford Motor Company's sales decline in the late 1920s was that Henry Ford, Sr., did not permit subordinates to make decisions. He had to confirm every purchase and make sure that he understood every production operation. Unfortunately, this took vital time away from activities that the chief of a large corporation should have been undertaking. Third, a manager must trust his or her subordinates. Delegation assumes that the manager trusts the subordinate to act responsibly. Many managers do not delegate, believing that the subordinates are not trained enough, cannot handle people, have not developed sufficient facts in the situation. Sometimes these considerations are true, but all too often they reflect the manager's distrust of subordinates and unwillingness to delegate decision-making authority.

Centralization–Decentralization

Whether authority should be concentrated or dispersed throughout the organization is a question not so much of what kind, but how much. Authority is a fundamental aspect of delegation. There is neither absolute centralization nor absolute decentralization. No one manager makes all decisions; total delegation would eliminate the need for managers. In other words, there is a continuum of centralization and decentralization. In addition, an organization may be relatively centralized in some functions and relatively decentralized in others.

Authority is delegated when a superior gives decision-making discretion to a subordinate. Clearly, supervisors should not delegate more authority that they have, nor should they delegate all of their authority, in effect passing on their job to their subordinates. The process of delegation involves the determination of results expected, the assignment of tasks and delegation of authority to accomplish them, and the responsibility for the task's accomplishments. In practice, these processes are impossible to split.

In summary, all the organizational design principles just discussed have been well-tested, and when implemented correctly, can reduce the likelihood that the organizational structure is the source of a crisis. Following these principles also increases the probability that the reorganization resulting from crises will prove successful. Unfortunately, violating these principles may be the cause of a crisis. For example, departmentalizing by product may mean that customers are overlooked, or, extending a manager's span of control beyond his or her capabilities may produce gaps in awareness, which are likely to lead to crisis.

CONTINGENCIES IN ORGANIZATIONAL DESIGN

As indicated by our previous discussion, a great deal of research has been invested in identifying the best ways to organize a company. However, there are many factors that are outside the control of the company and its management. It is these contingencies, that is, the unknowns, that cause a company the most difficulties, and often lead to crisis. The process of identifying the various contingencies and evaluating their importance is quite similar to the classification matrix that was created in Chapter 3. Moreover, it is our contention that by employing a contingency approach to organization design, we can accomplish two primary objectives: (1) create a reorganization process that parallels the crisis classification matrix, and (2) minimize the likelihood that mistakes in organization design will produce crisis.

CASE 5: THINGS GET COMPLICATED

Ben Enis started Evergreen Distributors nearly thirty years ago. Initially, the company distributed shampoo products to hair salons through the Cleveland metropolitan area. Over time, the company expanded its product lines to a full line of hair care products. In 1991, he began a chain of hair salons named Hair Etc. It was also about this same time that Ben realized he needed to plan for the future of his two sons, Greg and Ben Jr.

Ben Jr., the elder son, was a practicing attorney, living in Oxford, Ohio. Greg was three years younger and had worked in the family business, part time, since he was fourteen. His current title was manager of product development. Still, Ben wanted his family together, and convinced junior to return home with the title of general manager. Greg was very upset and lamented about the prodigal son getting all the attention. For the first three weeks after Ben Jr.'s return, he barely spoke to his brother. Then he thought about leaving the business and going out on his own.

Ben was in a terrible quandary, concerned that he had destroyed his sons' relationship.

Observation

This situation is quite common in family businesses. What criteria should be considered in situations such as these?

Defining the Contingency Approach

With the contingency approach to organizational design the manager needs to become familiar with the internal and external conditions facing the organization before deciding on the appropriateness of a particular organization structure. Effective organizational design results not from the use of just management principles, but from matching appropriate principles with the particular set of conditions facing the organization. Under certain conditions, classic bureaucratic rules and regulations may be very appropriate; under other conditions, they may not. Most of the research on contingency design theories has focused on two situational factors: technology and environmental uncertainty. One line of research has shown that differences in technology determine the most effective organizational design, while the second suggests that differences in environmental uncertainty and the demands for processing information are the crucial factors. These two approaches are compatible and can be combined into a general model of organizational design.

In the broadest sense, the environment is everything external to the organization's boundaries. However, it may be more useful to think of the environment as (1) the general environment, which affects all organizations in a given society, and (2) the specific task environment, which affects the individual organization more directly.

Many of the societal, or general, environmental forces that influences organizations include technological, educational, political, sociological, and economic factors. Frequently, managers take these conditions as given, with little recognition of how they affect the internal operations of organizations. These conditions set the general characteristics under which all organizations operate. An organization operating in the general environment may not be directly influenced by all of these conditions, nor can it respond to all of them.

The task environment comprises the specific forces relevant to the decision-making processes of the organization. The task environment is made up of groups beyond the organization's own boundaries that provide immediate inputs, exert pressures on decisions, or make use of the organization's outputs. The organization's task environment can be thought of as a subset of the general environment. Only the relevant conditions in the task environment affect the organization's performance.

The technological segment of the task environment has two parts. The first is the availability of the mechanical means for production of goods and services and possibly the replacement of human effort. This aspect emphasizes such things as automated production lines, computer systems, monitoring equipment, and other hardware. How these hardware are brought into the firm and set up are important tasks of the managers at the technical or production level. The technical advances within the organization cannot be carried any further than the technology available in the environment or created by the organization through its own research and development efforts.

But the economic or social costs of some technological advances may be too high for the organization. Large department stores, such as JC Penney, Sears, May Company, and K-Mart have their own data-processing centers for charge accounts, whereas a local store might still bill customers by a hand-posting method.

The second aspect of technology refers to the accumulated knowledge about the means to accomplish tasks. In this sense, technology is the skill and brains of individuals. It is the application of science to real-world problems. Accountants may use the computer in performing their tasks, but they also utilize the given knowledge of accounting procedures in accomplishing the task.

Characteristics of the Contingency Approach

The central theme of the contingency approach with respect to organizational design is that the degree of change and complexity in the task environment affects an organization's hierarchy, departmentation strategy, coordination mechanisms, and control systems. A firm that produces a stable product in a market with little technological innovation and relatively few competitors confronts a different organization—design problem than does a firm that provides a rapidly changing product or service in a growing, competitive market. The first environment is stable; the second, changing or uncertain. The degree of change in a firm's task environment may be thought of as a continuum ranging from stability to instability. These two states of the environment have substantial implications for the internal structure of the organization, the type of individual who is likely to be effective in the organization, and the type of management practices used in the organization. In general, firms operating in changing environments require internal organizational structures different from those of firms operating in stable environments.

The Stable Environment

A stable environment is characterized by the following:

1. products and services that have not changed much in recent years
2. lack of technological innovations
3. a stable set of competitors and customers, with a few new competitors
4. stable political, economic, and social conditions
5. consistent government policies toward regulation and taxation

Changes in a stable environment are relatively small. When they do occur, they have a minimal impact on the internal operations of the organizations. Top management can keep track of what is going on and make virtually all necessary policy decisions alone. Companies in the brewing, insurance, candle-making, coal-mining, glass container, and food-staples (e.g., flour and gelatin) industries operate in relatively stable environments. Although there may be slight changes in the product (e.g., the introduction of low-calorie beer in the brewing industry), these changes can be easily incorporated into the existing organizational structure.

The Changing Environment

A changing environment is characterized by the following:

1. products and services that have been changing moderately or continually
2. major technological innovations, which may make the old technology obsolete
3. an ever-changing set of actions by competitors and customers
4. unpredictable and changing governmental actions, reflecting political interactions between the public and various groups for consumer protection, pollution control, and civil rights
5. rapid changes in the values of a large number of individuals

Firms in this type of environment are likely to feel an ongoing need to adapt their internal structures to the environment. In an unstable environment, customers, prices, demands, and so on are changing. Products based on consumer preferences must be changed to meet new preferences and fads. Organizations in the electronics, pharmaceutical, and watch industries operate in changing, unstable environments.

CONTINGENCY APPROACHES TO ORGANIZATONAL DESIGN

Organizational structures will differ according to the conditions of their task environments. That is, the organization's subsystems (institutional, organizational, and technical) will differ, depending on whether the market and/or technology are stable or changing. Table 5.1 provides an overall framework for developing the contingency approach to the design of organizations. The two key factors are stability and homogeneity. Stability refers to the amount of changes in the dimensions in the organization's task environment over time. That is, are the number of customers, suppliers, manufacturing methods, and price structures stable or changing? Homogeneity, on the other hand, refers to the degree to which the task environment is segmented, whether there are numerous buyers, customers, and sellers, or few buyers, customers, and sellers. A heterogeneous task environment has many buyers and different types of customers and sellers; a homogeneous task environment, few buyers and limited types of customers and suppliers. The resulting four quadrants present different kinds of problems to the organization and therefore require different organizational structures.

Environmental Uncertainty

The degree of instability and uncertainty in the environment is another important situational variable that influences the appropriate type of organizational structure. Different organizational

Table 5.1
Contingency Designs of Organizations

Homogeneity	Stability	
	Stable	Changing
Homogeneous	1	11
Heterogeneous	111	1V

structures are required in order to cope with environmental uncertainty. Research is fairly consistent in indicating that organic structures tend to be most effective in uncertain environments while mechanistic structures are more effective in more stable environments. The classic study examining the effects of environmental uncertainty on organizational structure was conducted by Paul Lawrence and Jay Lorsch of Harvard University.

Lawrence and Lorsch examined organizations in three industries: plastics, packaged food products, and paper containers. These three industries were selected because significant differences were found in the degree of environmental uncertainty. The environment of the plastics firms was extremely uncertain because of rapidly changing technology and customer demand. Decisions were required about new products even though feedback about the accuracy of the decisions often involved considerable delay. In contrast, the paper container firms faced a highly certain environment. Only minor changes in technology had occurred in the previous twenty years, and these firms focused on producing high-quality, standardized containers and delivering them to the customer quickly. The consequences of decisions could be ascertained in a short period. Between these two extremes, the producers of packaged foods faced a moderately uncertain environment.

Differentiation and Integration

In analyzing how these firms interacted with their environments, Lawrence and Lorsch identified two key concepts: differentiation and integration. Differentiation is the degree of segmentation of the organizational system into subsystems, which is similar to the concepts of specialization of labor and departmentalization. However, differentiation also includes the behavioral attributes of employees in highly specialized departments. As noted earlier, members of highly specialized functional departments tend to adopt a rather narrow-minded, department-oriented focus that emphasizes the achievement of departmental goals rather than organizational goals.

The consequence of high differentiation is that greater coordination between departments is required. More time and resources must be devoted to achieving coordination, since the attitudes, goals, and work orientations among highly specialized departments differ so widely. Lawrence and Lorsch developed the concept of integration to refer to this coordinating activity. Integration was defined as the coordinating process of achieving unity of effort among the various subsystems to accomplish the organization's goals.

Responding to Uncertainty

Lawrence and Lorsch discovered significant relationships between the degree of environmental uncertainty and the amount of differentiation and integration used within each of the three industries. For example, the firms in the container industry faced a fairly certain environment, and they were fairly undifferentiated. Therefore, they tended to adopt a mechanistic structure. The most successful container companies were organized along functional lines with a highly centralized authority structure. Coordination was achieved through direct supervision with formal written schedules. A bureaucratic organization structure was consistent with the degree of environmental certainty of the container industry.

In the plastics industry, however, facing an extremely uncertain environment, the most successful plastics companies adopted organic structures. A highly unstable environment required these companies to have a highly differentiated structure with highly specialized internal departments of marketing, production, and research and development, to deal with the uncertainty in the external environment. Coordination was achieved through mutual adjustment, ad hoc teams that cut across departments, and special coordinators who served as liaisons between departments. The most successful plastics firms achieved high levels of differentiation plus high levels of integration to coordinate them.

The study of Lawrence and Lorsch contributes to our understanding of organizational design by showing the effects of environmental uncertainty on organizational structure. When the environment is highly uncertain, frequent changes require more information processing to achieve coordination, so special integrators and coordinating mechanisms become a necessary addition to the organization's structure. Sometime these integrators are called liaison personnel, brand managers, or product coordinators. Organizations that face a highly uncertain environment and a highly differentiated structure may have a fourth of their management personnel assigned to integration activities such as serving on committees, task forces, or in liaison roles. Organizations that face a very simple and stable environment, however, may not have anyone assigned to a full-time integration role.

Organizations in a dynamic and complex environment are unable to rely on traditional information processing and control techniques where all information is communicated through a chain of command. Changes in market demand, uncertain resources, and new technology disrupt the organization's plans and require adjustments while the task is being performed. Immediate adjustments to production schedules and task performance disrupt the organization. Coordination is made more difficult because it is impossible to forecast operations or revise standard operating rules or procedures. Organizations must obtain information that reflects the environmental changes.

ORGANIZATIONAL LIFE CYCLE

An important variable influencing organizational design is the age or maturity of the organization. However, it is not the chronological age that influences structure as much as the stage in the organization's life cycle. Organizations are born, grow larger, and get older, and they can die at any point in this life cycle.

Stages of Life Cycle

Organizational structure, leadership style, and administrative systems follow a predictable pattern of development and change as the organization processes through its life cycle. The stages are sequential in nature and follow a natural progression. Four major stages have been proposed to describe an organization's life cycle. Each stage is associated with a typical structure and a unique need that must be satisfied before the organization can move to the next stage.

1. *Entrepreneurial stage.* When an organization is first created, it starts with the entrepreneurial stage, and the emphasis is on creating a product that will survive in the marketplace. The entrepreneurs who start the organization typically devote their full energies to the technical activities of producing and marketing the product. While the organization is a small, one-person show, it adopts an organic structure. All structure and control are provided by the owner, whose energies are directed toward survival and the production of a single product or service. An organization needs dynamic leadership to move it from stage 1 to stage 2. Also, a strong manager is required who can introduce management techniques.

2. *Collectivity stage.* If the leadership crisis is resolved and the organization receives managerial direction and control, a formal organizational structure begins to emerge. Departments are established based on a division of labor along with a hierarchy of authority. The structure, however, is a highly organic structure where members interact freely. Long hours of work are contributed by employees who are motivated by a sense of commitment and involvement. The goals and direction for the organization are provided by a strong, charismatic leader. To move an organization from stage 2 to stage 3, the organization has a need for delegation with control. Some organizations experience an

autonomy crisis when top managers who were successful because of their strong leadership and vision do not want to relinquish any of their responsibility. Consequently, the organization must find mechanisms to coordinate and control departments that are allowed increasing levels of authority without direct supervision from the top.

3. *Formalization stage.* As the organization enters the formalization period, during the middle of its life, bureaucratic characteristics emerge. Staff support groups are added to the organization along with formal procedures and a clear division of labor. Top managers must now focus their attention primarily on issues of strategy and planning and leave the day-to-day operation of the firm to lower-level managers. Incentive systems, such as executive bonuses and profit sharing, may be implemented to motivate managers to work toward the overall good of the company. If the organization can successfully implement coordination and control systems, it will continue to grow and operate effectively. For the organization to advance from stage 3 to stage 4, it must resolve the problem of excessive formality and bureaucratic red tape. Organizations tend to proliferate systems and programs that can overwhelm the organization.

4. *Elaboration stage.* If the organization can eliminate unnecessary bureaucratic procedures, it can continue to grow and enter the elaboration stage. Here the organization is large and bureaucratic with extensive control systems, rules, and procedures. Managers learn to work within the bureaucracy without adding to it. The pervasiveness of bureaucratic procedures may reduce the effectiveness of the organization and force it to decline. The energies of individuals throughout the organization often focus more on maintaining the organization than on innovative and creative ideas. Innovation is formally institutionalized and assigned to the research and development department. Creative ideas that come from elsewhere in the organization are often ignored. For the organization to stay at this stage and not decline or die, it needs to be periodically revitalized. The renewal process tends to occur every few years when the organization slips out of alignment with environment, and the problems are so severe that members feel a strong need for change. During these periods of change, top managers are often replaced by new managers with fresh ideals.

Organizational Decline

Organizations are designed to grow, and there are inherent forces within the organization that naturally push for the organization to grow and expand. However, there are also environmental forces that threaten the survival of the organization. Indeed, some environmental forces require organizations to decline. Changing population patterns have reduced the number of students in schools and patients in urban hospitals. Foreign competition has closed

steel mills and copper mines. Certain industries, especially automotive companies, have laid off record numbers of employees in
response to a recessionary economy and decreased demand. Organizational decline, sometimes called downsizing, is a cutback in
the size of the organization's workforce, profits, budget, or clients.

Managing an organization during a period of decline is much more
difficult and usually much more unpleasant than managing a growing organization. In periods of growth, budgets are loose, new people
are added, resources are plentiful, and bad decisions do not seem
so serious. During periods of decline, when resources are scarce,
faithful long-term employees may need to be terminated, the employees who remain are unhappy, and bad decisions can sometimes
be catastrophic.

During periods of decline, organizations are often required to
make two types of adjustments: recentralization and reallocation.

1. *Recentralization*. Decentralized authority often must be withdrawn during periods of decline. Decisions about the future of the organization
   and the types of adjustments that must be made to enable it to survive must be made by top management. Some departments may have
   to be eliminated, employees may have to be laid off, pay may be cut,
   and resources may be redirected. These decisions usually create such
   serious disagreement and debate that it is best for them to be made by
   top managers exercising centralized authority.

2. *Reallocation*. Organizations in decline are often required to eliminate
   some of their products or services. Low-priority management programs
   may also need to be eliminated. Making these decisions means reallo-
   cating resources among those who remain. The way the resources are
   allocated will reflect the survival strategy of top management.

CRISES ORGANIZATIONS

Having laid the necessary groundwork, it is now possible to suggest an organizational process that may prevent and minimize crisis. For the sake of consistency, we present this process in the context
of proactive and reactive processes, a dyad employed throughout
this book.

A Proactive Organization

Recall that a proactive organization strategy would attempt to anticipate possible contingencies and plan accordingly. The primary concern throughout this process is the role played by possible crisis.

A four-step organizational process is recommended: (1) Follow the
principles of organization design, (2) employ a contingency approach

in actual design, (3) overlay the contingency structure onto the classification matrix for crisis management, and (4) recommend an organizational structure appropriate for the contingencies identified.

Follow the Principles of Organization Design

Most of this chapter provided a review of principles developed in designing an organization. Therefore, an overview of these principles suggests the following:

1. A clear structure of roles must be designed and maintained by management. This includes a clear concept of the major activities and duties involved, a clear understanding of the relationship of that role with others, and a mechanism that provides the needed information to carry out the duties.
2. It is best to departmentalize the organization based on function, place, product, and customers.
3. Organization coordination is accomplished through a clear statement of the unity of command and an estimate of span of control.
4. A clear authority structure makes the division of work and its coordination possible. This includes a definition and assignment of responsibility, accountability, delegation of authority, and assessment of centralization–decentralization deemed appropriate.

Employ a Contingency Approach in Organizational Design

A contingency approach simply attempts to identify all unknown factors that might influence the organization and make necessary adjustments. It also assumes that the adjustments will reflect the organizational principles employed. In general, two situational types of variables tend to be the focus of contingency assessment: technology and environment uncertainty (general and task). Thus, we can create a contingency matrix that includes all these variables and parallels the crisis classification matrix. Moreover, the specific organizational design elements impacted by the contingency matrix include the following: the organization's hierarchy, the departmentation strategy, coordination mechanisms, and control system.

Overlay the Contingency Structure onto the Crisis Classification Matrix

For our discussion on organizational principles and contingency design to have value to the crisis manager, it is necessary to blend organizational design issues and crisis. We begin by providing an expanded version of the contingency design matrix discussed earlier in this chapter. This new matrix is shown in Figure 5.1. Essentially, stability and homogeneity, the two elements of organizational dynamics, are now on the outer ridge of the crisis classification matrix. Although not a perfect match, the organizational criteria do follow the rationale of the crisis matrix. For example, Level 4 of the crisis classification matrix now includes an organizational structure that has changing stability and is heterogeneous, suggesting the most dynamic organizational structure possible. There is also an implicit suggestion that the organizational structure is a likely source of crisis.

Recommend an Organizational Structure Appropriate for the Contingencies Identified

The ultimate payoff is to employ what we know about organizational design and contingencies, combine this information with Figure 5.1, and produce a set of organizational design recommendations. To simplify our discussion, we begin by dividing the classification

Figure 5.1
Expanded Crisis Contingency Design Matrix

STABILITY			CHANGING		STABLE	
Time Pressure			Intense		Minimal	
Threat Level	Degree of Control		*Low*	*High*	*Low*	*High*
	Response Options					
Low	*Many*		(4) Level 2	(3) Level 1	(2) Level 1	(1) · Level 0
	Few		(8) Level 3	(7) Level 2	(6) Level 2	(5) Level 1
High	*Many*		(12) Level 3	(10) Level 2	(10) Level 2	(9) Level 1
	Few		(16) Level 4	(14) Level 3	(14) Level 3	(13) Level 2

matrix (Figure 5.1) into four quadrants: QI is cells 1, 2, 5, 6; QII is cells 3, 4, 7, 8; QIII is cells 9, 10, 13, 14; and QIV is cells 11, 12, 15, 16.

To illustrate how this might work, let's look at QI. QI has the following characteristics: stable or homogeneous organization dynamics, minimal time pressure, and low threat level. Companies operating in this quadrant would best employ a somewhat mechanistic organizational design, which changes little over time and requires few adjustments. In contrast, QIV would necessitate a more organic organizational design, requiring a high ability to change as new information dictates. Adaptive planning is part of the organization structure.

Following the process of designing an organization structure that is responsive to the crisis contingency matrix first described, it is necessary to create an implementation structure. That is, a mechanism must be put in place that both monitors potential crisis and implements possible solutions. This mechanism, or organization structure, can be formal and/or informal. The latter would be most appropriate in a small organization, where the observances of employees may prove adequate in spotting and reporting problems. In such cases, training employees to look for problems and then rewarding them for their responses might do the job.

In larger companies, or companies with greater serious potential crisis, a more elaborate implementation structure might be necessary. This could include formal committees, perhaps categorized by customer type or geography. It might mean designating and training a spokesperson who is responsible for communicating to the media. The use of technology, such as the Internet, may also be a formal response mechanism. Several more examples are discussed in later chapters.

A Reactive Organization

Regardless of the best efforts of crisis managers, there will be events that cannot be anticipated and a reactive organization structure is needed. In these instances creating a crisis-response organization is often necessary. If the crisis is viewed as minor, it is likely that the proactive crisis structure can handle the response and no additional reorganization would be required. For example, a major power outage may be unusual in a city that has few outages, but likely can be handled by an effective organization structure. However, a company that experiences a sexual harassment suit that involves a senior manager may have to create a response team to handle this crisis. In the latter instance, the more traditional recommendations would apply:

- Designate the members of the crisis-management team.
- Identify the likely company representative to handle media relations.
- Determine the message, target, and media outlets that would be used in implementing the crisis-communication plan.

Conceivably, the response to these recommendations would be handled through the proactive organization structure, thereby reducing the steepness of the learning curve.

CONCLUSION

One of the primary reasons why organizations have crises and don't deal with them effectively is that they are poorly organized. There is a right way and a wrong way to do this. This chapter discussed the right ways and suggested that subscribing to them is a crucial part of proactive crisis management.

6

Putting Controls in Place

Experience is the name everyone gives to their mistakes.
Oscar Wilde

QUESTIONABLE CHOICES

The E. C. Kraft Company builds ovens for commercial use. These include bakeries, pizza restaurants, and pie shops. They have been in business since 1968, and the business is now managed by Charles Kraft, E. C. Kraft's only son. Growth has averaged about 4 percent annually and they have evolved from a regional business, with Mr. Kraft doing all the sales, to a national business, with a field sales force of six, an interactive Web site, and a toll-free number as part of their trade ads.

The growth during the last three years has been so rapid that management has never been able to put measures of control in place. For instance, they have no idea whether the sales force is cost effective, nor do they know how many dollars of sales are being generated through the Web site. Everyone is figuring out what needs to be done, and how they fit into getting it done, as they go along.

Crisis is very much about control. When we have control of our environment, crises are far less likely to occur. An organization that is out of control is doomed to a life of putting out fires. Consequently, understanding the nature of control and how it is implemented greatly enhances the success of crisis management.

NATURE OF CONTROL

In its broadest sense, control refers to the process by which a person, group, or organization consciously determines or influences what another person, group, or organization will do. Within organizations, and society in general, reactions to the word "control" is very negative; often being interpreted to imply restraining, coercing, delimiting, directing, enforcing, watching, manipulating, and inhibiting. This is partially due to the strong belief in Western cultural values such as individualism and democracy; which appear to be inconsistent with the notion of control. Individualism is based on self-control and some external controls, such as certain government laws.

Some laws serve to limit the imposition of control by one group or institution over another. The Bill of Rights acts as a mechanism to limit (control) the actions of the state on its citizenry. This type of mechanism might be thought of as preventive control. Preventive control refers to mechanisms designed to minimize the need for taking corrective action. In organizations, rules and regulations and training-and-development programs function primarily as preventive controls. Rules and regulations limit the actions employees can take to reach the organization's goals. It is usually assumed that if the employees comply, the goals of the organization are more likely to be achieved. Employees are kept focused on the specific goals that management and/or ownership sets for the company as a whole instead of each focusing on his or her own perception of what they should do for the company.

The more common view of managerial and organizational control emphasizes a process of corrective control, or mechanisms designed to return the individual or department to some predetermined condition. For example, management might believe that theft by some employees has increased. To change this situation, management might now require all employees to enter and depart the building from a common entry and exit area, as well as post a security guard.

Managerial control can be both preventive and corrective in nature, and distinctions between the two types may be found within a single managerial practice. Thus reward–punishment practices may prevent deviations by promising rewards for compliance, as well as attempting to correct deviations by providing punishments or with-holding rewards. A salesperson may be promised a bonus if sales go above a certain level and threatened with dismissal if sales fall below a certain level.

Uses of Controls

Formal control systems, strategies, and practices are put to many uses within organizations:

1. Controls may be used to standardize performance. This might be accomplished by supervisory inspections, written procedures, or production schedules.
2. Controls may be used to protect an organization's assets from theft, waste, or misuse. Record-keeping requirements, auditing procedures, and division of responsibilities are some of the tactics of control here.
3. Controls may be used to standardize the quality of products or services offered by an organization. This might be attained through employee training, inspections, statistical quality control, and incentive systems.
4. Controls may be established to limit the amount of authority that can be exercised by various organizational positions and levels. The limits on discretion may be expressed in job descriptions, policy directives, rules, and auditing systems.
5. Controls for measuring and directing employee performance are common. Merit-rating systems, direct supervisory observation, and reports on output or scrap loss per employee are illustrative.
6. Managerial planning is a major means of preventive control. The process of setting goals helps to define the appropriate scope and direction of the members' behaviors to achieve the desired results.

There are, of course, many other uses of formal controls in organizations. Formal controls are spread throughout every aspect of organizations; control is needed to ensure the stability and adaptability of all organizations. Even so, there remain many unresolved issues, for example, the amount of control the organization needs to exercise, the appropriate basis of an organization's control system (whether reward or punishment centered), and the types of control strategies considered acceptable by the organization's members. Issues of organizational and societal control are intimately related to questions of values. In the People's Republic of China, for example, the intensive socialization of the people, along with the unique Chinese cultural heritage, have led to widespread agreement among the citizenry as to the right of the government to control many aspects of individuals' behavior.

Economics of Control

Formal controls should be recognized as means to help the organization achieve its desired results. The costs of formal control systems relative to their benefits must be assessed in the same manner as other organizational processes. Analysis of the economics of control systems, strategies, and practices involves three basic questions:

1. What are the costs versus benefits of various amounts of formal controls?
2. What are the cost-benefit relationships of alternative strategies for controlling the same activity?
3. At what point or for what activities should controls be used?

The economic benefit of a formal control system is the difference between its costs and the improvement in performance it creates. For example, when the quality of output is unsatisfactory, is it more economical to do the following: (1) lower the span of control so that superiors can more closely supervise their subordinated, (2) create a system of worker rewards that would increase with increases in quality, (3) substitute machines for humans, or (4) change the points or location of controls to detect errors earlier?

CORRECTIVE MODEL OF CONTROL

The corrective model of control refers to the process of detecting and correcting deviations from preestablished goals or standards. It places heavy reliance on feedback and reaction to what has already happened. As shown in Figure 6.1 the development and maintenance of a corrective model of control consists of six interconnected steps: (1) define the subsystem (e.g., an individual or department), (2) identify characteristics to be measured, (3) set standards, (4) collect information, (5) make comparisons, and (6) diagnose and implement corrections.

Define the Subsystem

A formal control process might be created and maintained for a single employee, a department, or a whole organization. The controls could focus on specific inputs, production processes, or outputs. Controls on inputs often limit the degree of variance from standards in the resources utilized within the production process of the organization. This serves to reduce the uncertainty about the quality and quantity of inputs into the production process. For example, at the Joseph P. Schlitz breweries, elaborate controls (in-

Figure 6.1
Corrective Model of Control

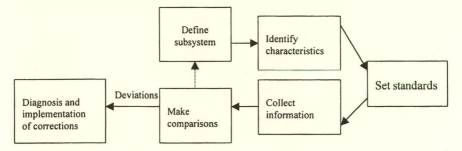

cluding human inspections and laboratory testing) are used to make sure that the water and grains used in the production of beer meet predetermined standards. The production process (production subsystem) consists of a web of controls: length of time for cooking the brew, temperature in the vats, sampling of the brew, laboratory testing of it in each stage of the production process, inspection of the beer prior to final packing, and so forth. Controls on the final output of goods and services could range from levels of inventories to monitoring consumer attitudes toward acceptance of the company's goods and services.

Identify Characteristics

The types of information that can and should be obtained about the subsystem must be identified. The establishment of a formal corrective-control process requires an early assessment of certain questions: What information characteristics are feasible from a technical standpoint? What are the economic costs versus expected benefits associated with obtaining information on each characteristic? Does variation in the characteristics make any difference in the essential performance goals or objectives of the subsystem?

Set Standards

Management should establish standards for each of the characteristics being measured. Standards are the criteria for evaluating the activities being undertaken by the subsystem.

There are often interrelationships between standards, thus requiring considerable coordination between organizational departments. For example, a consulting firm with goals of providing only the highest-quality services will need to develop an elaborate network of standards for screening its personnel. These selection standards might include a minimum of a master's degree, three years of applicable experience, and the like.

Management is increasingly developing control systems based on performance standards, or statements of the results that exist when performance is satisfactory. For example, American Airlines has established the following types of standards (there are also others) for judging the quality of performance for each of its airport ticket offices. The specific quantitative levels for each of these types of standards approximate the following:

1. *Waiting time.* At least 85 percent of the customers arriving at an airport ticket counter shall be waited on within five minutes.
2. *Baggage mishandlings.* Baggage mishandlings by airport ticket sales personnel, skycaps, and ticket-lift agents shall not exceed one per twenty checked and rechecked bags.
3. *Customer impact.* At least 90 percent of airport customer contacts shall be rated acceptable.
4. *Posted flight-arrival times.* At least 95 percent of the flight-arrival times posted in the "will arrive" columns on the arrival board shall be accurate to the degree that the actual arrivals will be within fifteen minutes of the time posted.

Collect Information

The collection of information refers to the means used to obtain measurements on each of the designated characteristics. Information could be collected through human (observations by a supervisor) or mechanical (a counting device) means. Information may also be collected by the individual or group whose performance is to be controlled. In some cases, this can result in a loss of meaningful control, especially if money can be diverted to satisfy an individual's or group's personal needs or if those needs aren't being adequately met. In 1995, for example, the new president of Union Planters National Bank of Memphis, Tennessee, found considerable corruption among eight executives and even some clerks. Three of the former employees were sent to jail and several others were indicted. The president claims that executives were getting payoffs in exchange for making shaky multimillion-dollar loans. Other employees were found to be simply embezzling money. Why did this happen? According to the new president, the lack of formal controls combined with low pay scales encouraged dishonesty. To solve these problems, he gave a hefty across-the-board pay increase to the bank employees and installed a new control system to prevent shaky loans and detect corruption quickly.

Often employees are motivated to distort or conceal data that can be used as a basis for punishing, demoting, or criticizing themselves. For example, if American Airlines relied on its airport ticket counter employees for the basis data used to calculate performance standards, we might expect some motivation to conceal or distort the data. This might become especially troublesome if the data were then used as a basis for punishing the employees.

Managers often create special departments to act as information collectors by auditing certain activities of other departments. Thus a personnel department might collect data to see that the standards regarding pay raises are being met. Similarly, a controller's department might collect and analyze information to see that expenditures of funds are completed according to certain standards.

Make Comparisons

The process of making comparisons refers to determining whether differences exist between the activities and results that are actually taking place and what should be occurring. This process involves comparing the information collected with the established standards, which might be contained in written rules, computer programs, or on tap in the manager's memory. A purely comparative activity might occur when a graduate assistant of a professor does the following: (1) obtains the output of student scores on a multiple-choice test from the college scoring center, (2) compares these scores with the professor's standards, (3) determines the extent to which the students' scores (performances) differ from the standards, but (4) then gives these analyses to the professor for the evaluation of grades because the results are not consistent with the established standards.

If no difference between what is actually taking place and what should be taking place shows up, the department normally continues to function without any intervention.

Diagnose and Implement Corrections

The final stage in the control process is to assess how significant the differences are between what we wanted to accomplish and what we actually do accomplish. For example, comparisons of two training programs might indicate that Program A produced a very high level of technical competency, but a pooor understanding of the process itself. Program B did just the opposite. It would then be up to the manager to determine which strengths and weaknesses are most important to the company, its level of productivity and predilection to avoid crises.

He or she might decide that Program A is best and that several key elements of Program B can be incorporated. This is implementation.

SOME CONTINGENCIES INFLUENCING
THE CONTROL PROCESS

Power

Different control systems, strategies, and practices are closely linked to different kinds and combinations of power used within the organization. Each type of power describes a different relationship between the person subjected to power and the person exercising that power. A general definition of power is "the ability to limit choice," and the types of power by which choice can be limited differ significantly. An organization may use different combinations of five types of power—reward, coercive, legitimate, referent, and expert.

Reward power refers to a person's or group's perception that another person or group has the ability to provide varying amounts and types of rewards. A common example of this is the superior's granting different pay increases for different levels of performance by subordinates. Managements have often resisted the formation of unions in their organizations because collective bargaining tends to reduce their discretion to reward employees based on different levels of performance. Within business organizations, this is probably the most important type of power used to achieve control over people. It is usually considered desirable to base rewards on performance measures. This is because there should be greater motivation to perform well, especially when the job is not personally satisfying or rewarding.

Coercive power refers to a person's or group's perception that another person or group has the ability to administer punishments. In the political system, obvious forms of coercive power include physical punishments such as inflicting pain, deformity, or death, and the forceful control over basic human needs. Coercive power in business organizations is commonly expressed through such means as dismissals (or threats of dismissal), demotions, and social pressure.

One of the basic problems with control systems based on coercive power is that they tend to create alienation, withdrawal, aggressive hostilities in those subjected to them. Thus a paradox is created. Coercive power is often justified by management as necessary to gain compliance in order for the organization to attain its goals. But the excessive use of coercive power, as perceived by the employees, may serve to reduce their motivation to comply. It may actually motivate them to withdraw from their work by becoming passive and indifferent participants, creating an even more difficult control problem. To reduce their frustrations, they may also militantly strike back. The massive unionization in the late 1930s was partially a reaction to the coercive power used by some business organizations. In the public sector, some segments of the population view court-ordered busing as an exercise of coercive power by the courts and other government agencies.

Legitimate power, based on the values held by an individual, exists when one person or group believes it is rightful or desirable for another person or group to influence their actions. Thus faculty members are usually viewed as having a legitimate right to assign students grades based on academic performance.

An employee who believes in the institutions of private property and the basic framework of a free-enterprise system may feel that the superior's control of his or her behavior to obtain profits is quite appropriate. In contrast, an employee who believes in public ownership and control of the means of production may interpret managerial controls over his or her work as a form of exploitation. In this case, the superior would be perceived as having little legitimate power, and this would make the superior's control of such an individual much more difficult.

Referent power is based on the desire of one individual or group to identify with or be like another person or group. It is often expressed by copying the actions, style, and beliefs of that individual or group. A manager who defines getting ahead as obtaining successively higher positions in an organization may be especially prone to control through referent power. This individual, placed under an effective manager, may rapidly develop many of the same skills and perceptions as his or her superior. This occurs because of the strong psychological identification with the superior and the need for recognition from that person. In such cases, referent power may be functional for both the individual and the organization.

Expert power refers to a person's or group's perception that another person or group has greater knowledge or expertise and is thus worthy of following. A person might gain expert power through special experience, training, reputation, or demonstrated ability. Professional programs in colleges and universities (e.g., business, engineering, and law) generally create within their students the power of expertise. Many positions in business organizations rely on various types of expertise, for example, engineers, accountants, statisticians, market researchers, skilled tradesmen, and professional managers.

Technology

The types of controls found in the technical subsystem of an organization are influenced by the type of technology used: unit production, mass production, or continuous process. Unit-production technology is the custom manufacturing of individual items, such as an aircraft carrier, nuclear power plant, skyscraper, or custom house. The control system here is likely to emphasize the employee's self-control, managerial surveillance, and control through detailed plans. There is likely to be only a slight use of mechanical controls.

Mass-production technology refers to the manufacture of large volumes of identical or similar goods, such as automobiles, baby food, or toothpaste. With this technology, the control system shifts toward impersonal mechanisms and reliance on rules and regulations and mechanical controls, for example, assembly-line-paced work.

Continuous-process technology is characterized by an ongoing flow of activities for transforming inputs into outputs, with virtually all physical activities being performed by machines. The workers do not so much handle the material itself as monitor the workflow via dials and diagnose work in the production process. Gasoline, milk, soft drinks, and many chemicals are manufactured by continuous-process technology. This type of technology relies heavily on mechanical and other impersonal controls. Thus machines are likely to control other machines, and these controls are based primarily on the corrective model of control presented earlier.

Level in the Formal Hierarchy

Structural characteristics of organizations can also affect the control system. The concern here is with different combinations of the amount and distribution of control at different levels in the organization's hierarchy. The distribution-of-control variable refers to the relative control by each level in the hierarchy over the activities of the organization. For example, how much control is exercised by top management relative to first-level supervision? The amount-of-control variable refers to the quantity of control by each group or level within the organization. For example, how much of the total control of the organization is exercised by top management, middle management, first-level supervision, and the production workers?

Managers have traditionally been concerned with distribution of control in organizations, that is, who is to have the right to exercise particular types of controls. But the total amount of control in an organization may have a bearing on its effectiveness as well. The total amount of control refers to the amount of control held by all groups throughout the organization. If a union has a low amount of control over members' behavior, its effectiveness in bargaining with management is likely to be reduced. Organizational effectiveness might also be influenced by the degree of agreement among the participants with respect to (1) their perceptions of the actual distribution and the amount of control and (2) their values as to what the distribution and amount of control ought to be. Considerable differences in these perceptions and values could be a source of internal organizational conflicts and dissatisfaction. Consistent with the contingency approach, there is no single ideal control system. Rather, the ideal system will depend on such factors as the technology used to produce the goods and services, values of the participants, organizational structure, power system, and degree of uncertainty and change experienced by the organization.

STRATEGIES OF CONTROL

In this section we will discuss six strategies of control: human-input control, reward–punishment system, formal structure, policies and rules, budgets, and mechanical controls. These strategies are not necessarily mutually exclusive. Indeed, the control of many activities often requires the use of two (or more) of these strategies at the same time. A combination and interweaving of control strategies probably creates a synergistic effect. In other words, greater control is achieved through a combination of strategies than if each strategy operated independently.

For the most part, our discussion emphasizes the strategies for controlling an organization's employees and managers. There are two reasons for this. First, for most organizations, labor is the greatest cost factor. Second, controlling labor may provide an effective, although sometimes indirect, means of achieving control over the other resources used to create the organization's outputs.

The form and design of each of these formal control strategies depend on many human variables, some of which we shall discuss here.

Human Input

To increase the probability of effectiveness in any type of organization, managers must control the instability, variability, and spontaneity of individual acts. Selection techniques provide for the screening of personnel for each position in the organization. Training programs provide for changes in the skills and attitudes of employees. These are two of the means for controlling unwanted kinds of variability. If the organization is to prosper, selection and training controls need to be utilized (prisons and custodial institutions are notable exceptions).

Considerable managerial discretion usually exists over the policies and content of employee selection and training. Much popular interest has been directed at selection and training to determine (1) the extent to which many of the policies employed accomplish their purpose (a technical question), (2) the legalities of some of these policies, especially with respect to personnel selection on the basis of race, sex, creed, or national origin (social and political questions), and (3) the desirability of using certain selection and training approaches, such as personality tests or sensitivity-training groups (ethical and social questions).

Selection controls are used in hiring people and promoting or transferring employees within the organization. The conditions in the external labor market are likely to have considerable influence on the types and level of selection controls. In a scarce labor market, few candidates are available, and the organization may find it necessary to lower its standards or number of controls. To offset the reduced quality of the work force, management might increase its training emphasis or redesign the jobs.

The use of controls in the selection process depends partly on the amount of decision-making discretion and power that the person is supposed to exercise. Two interrelated aspects of the discretion and power in the position to be filled are important. First, how much can the individual's decisions harm or aid the welfare of the organization? Second, how much formal power will the individual have over the use and allocation of the organization's resources? For example, controls are minimal in the selection of file clerks compared to those used in the selection of marketing executives who develop sales strategies, control budgets, and supervise others.

Training is the organization's conscious attempt to change the skills, knowledge, attitudes, values, or motivations of individuals to help achieve its goals. In most types of training, the interests of the individual and the organization are probably compatible. Many professional programs (such as business, engineering, and law) conducted by colleges and universities serve the interests of both the students and the organizations that are likely to employ them. These professional programs provide more than a specific set of skills and technical knowledge. The student is exposed to various social controls, both formal and informal, that can serve to influence individual attitudes, motivations, and values. Similarly, company orientation and developmental programs are usually concerned with forming or modifying attitudes to make them consistent with the needs of the organization. Management development, in contrast to technical and skill training, is often intended to develop in an employee a sense of commitment of the philosophy and goals of a business organization. Blue-collar employees in routine positions are likely to have little exposure to such programs. Only occupants of discretionary positions, such as those held by managers and specialists, are usually exposed to intensive development programs.

CASE 6: TRAINING IS DEBATABLE

Machinist Union 749 is one of the most powerful labor unions in Phoenix, Arizona. Overall, they have more than 1,100 paying members, earning salaries ranging from $16.95 per hour to $31.55 per hour. They have members working in 162 businesses throughout the Phoenix Metropolitan area. Most of their contract negotiations will take place during the next two years.

One of the most important issues in future negotiations appears to be training. One difference, however, is that training is being defined much more broadly than in the past. Machinists have very uncertain futures, with many of their skills being replaced by computer automation. Therefore, training for members of the union now includes training in more marketable skills, job seeking skills, and at least one area outside their immediate job. Management calculates that this new training will cost twice as much as the current programs.

Observation

Who should determine the training needs of the organization? Management? Employees?

The amount of effort an organization puts into conditioning individual values, attitudes, and goals ranges from relative indifference to intensive indoctrination. Chaos and instability might result if managers had highly incompatible goals, values, and attitudes. At the other extreme is the absolute conformity of the "organization man" stereotype. Intensive conditioning may lead to a static organization, one that is unable to adapt and change. For example, it has been widely reported that in both the Johnson and Nixon administrations, there was little tolerance of members within the total policy group who challenged the existing Vietnam policy and the assumption on which it was based.

The ideal strategy might be to employ deliberate conditioning to create unity without conformity. Many Management by Objectives (MBO) programs and decentralization strategies may provide the means of achieving unity without conformity. This occurs by first encouraging the open discussion of goals both written and unwritten, that are being pursued. Then an effort is made to reach agreement on the objectives that should be pursued. Finally, the individuals are given some discretion for working toward the objectives in a manner of their own choosing.

Reward–Punishment Systems

Formal systems of rewards and punishments are another control strategy use to direct individuals to fulfilling the requirements of the organization. As suggested earlier, there are wide variations in the form and effectiveness of such systems. Here we present a broad framework showing the range of reward-and-punishment combinations from an extremely mechanistic organization to an extremely organic system.

An extremely mechanistic organization attempts to control employee behavior through punishment and the individual's fear of being deprived of the few rewards that are provided by the organization. Such organizations are prisons, prisoner-of-war camps, custodial mental hospitals, and some business firms. The members of these organizations usually have a strong desire to escape from such organizations. The managers of these organizations often have little discretion in selecting their members and spend little money on formal training programs.

In the more typical business mechanistic system, however, there are attempts to control employees by emphasizing the exchange of extrinsic rewards in return for the performance of certain designated tasks. Extrinsic rewards are in the form of wages, pension plans, some types of status symbols (size of office, access to information, etc.), and job security. At times, the typical mechanistic system may rely on certain forms of punishments, such as demotions or dismissal. Many business organizations, farmers' cooperatives, some peacetime military organizations, and labor unions make use of this pattern of rewards and punishments.

In a highly organic management system, by contrast, there is an attempt to control employee behavior through the use of intrinsic rewards (i.e., satisfying work), self-control (personal sense of responsibility for one's work), interpersonal control (control through advice and suggestions by those with the expertise), and a reasonable degree of extrinsic rewards. Organizations approaching this pattern of control include research and development organizations (especially for managers and skilled personnel), colleges and universities (especially for faculty and administrators), and voluntary and professional associations.

As suggested in the previous description of moderately mechanistic through organic management systems, punishment is not likely to be a dominant control mechanism in most organizations. This is because it is simply not a very effective method of controlling behavior. However, individuals and organizations do occasionally use punishment (or are perceived as using it) for the following types of reasons:

1. It may suppress undesired behavior when all other means for modifying it have failed.
2. It may be seen as an effective deterrent even when it has little actual deterrent effect on the specific individuals who have been punished (punishment may reinforce conformity to the prevailing standards by the larger group of members).
3. The taking way of rewards may become psychologically indistinguishable from punishments (e.g., failure to receive a regular increase in salary may be considered a penalty).
4. The desire of individuals to get even for harm done to them may cause them to seek to punish others; thus revenge or retribution may itself become a source of reward.

A strike may represent a means for management and labor to exchange punishments and withdraw the rewards that are usually forthcoming in their relationship. The power of each party to punish the other by refusing to cooperate is occasionally a mutually disastrous experience. This seemed to be one reason for the failure of the Newark, New Jersey, *Evening News* in September 1972. In 1970, when Media General, Inc., acquired the newspaper for $24 million, the new management felt that the paper was overstaffed and tried to fire 50 editorial writers.

Policies and Rules

Policies and rules, another major means for exercising control over many organizational activities and functions, define the discretion available in a position or unit as well as indicate mandatory actions. A policy is a guide for carrying out action, and it is generally qualitative, conditional, and relational; that is, it is general rather than specific and expresses a condition or relation. The verbs used in stating policies are to maintain, to follow, to provide, to assist, to use, and so forth. Thus a policy might be worded: "Promotions will be based on merit."

A rule is a specific course of action or conduct that must be followed. It is established to create uniformity of action and may or may not be prohibitive. An example of a rule is, "Courses may be dropped by the student up through the third week of classes without a grade being assigned."

Flexibility is probably the most basic difference between policies and rules. Policies tend to be made by managers at higher organizational levels, whereas rule making often occurs at all organizational levels. Policy making at General Motors, for example, is the responsibility of the executive and finance committees, which are composed entirely of the company's directors. Subcommittees of the executive and finance committees include representation from major divisions and departments of the entire organization and frequently develop rules to implement the firm's general policies.

Rules may have both desirable and undesirable consequences for the formal organization. The following summarizes the major consequences of rules:

1. Rules reflect authority, and thus they structure relationships and ensure action consistent with the organization's purposes. For example, rules may define the relative authority of the personnel department and other managers in the organization with respect to the hiring of employees.

2. Although rules may be called on when individual competence or commitment is low, they may reinforce apathy by defining the minimum acceptable standard for subordinates. For example, there may be a rule specifying that employees who do not average 300 units of output per week will be subject to a disciplinary layoff. This type of rule may well create negative attitudes toward management and simply motivate the employees to produce 300 units and no more.

3. By focusing undue attention on standards of behavior and operating procedures, rules may inadvertently result in a means–end reversal for the organization. This could cause impersonal relations with clients, inflexibility, and resistance to innovation. Following a rule becomes a goal or end rather than a means to an end. For example, a rule may state that the organization will stop serving its clientele at 5:00 P.M. When one of the authors was standing in line at a library on a Saturday afternoon, the clock struck 5:00 P.M.. Even though several people protested, the clerk cited the rule and refused to check out any more books.

4. Rules may receive additional authority from the desire of subordinates to structure working conditions and relationships in a predictable fashion. This creates a domino effect (rules beget rules) as management attempts to deal with hostile worker groups. For example, there may be rules specifying the number of vacation days employees receive

based on number of years worked. But conflict might arise between management and workers over how this vacation time should be taken—all at once or spread out. If specific requests cannot be worked out cooperatively and with some give and take on both sides, an elaborate network of formal rules may be developed to specify how vacation time can be taken.

Budgets

Budgets set up targets desired by the organization in the future. These target characteristics are usually expressed in terms of dollars. Nonfinancial characteristics, such as production budgets expressed in units (hours of labor per unit or output, machine downtime per thousand hours of running time, and the like), may also be used.

The control aspect of budgets may be either preventive or corrective. In the corrective model, considerable effort may be expended in identifying deviations from the budget. The reported deviations serve as a basis for subsequent managerial action aimed at identifying the causes for the deviation or evaluating whether the budget itself should be changed.

The power of a budget, especially as a preventive control mechanism, depends on viewing it as a bargain or informal contract that has been agreed to by all parties. One study investigated this and other issues by mailing a comprehensive questionnaire to lower-level supervisors to obtain their views about how the company budget was used. They were asked, "Do you feel that frequently budgets or standards are a club held over the head of the supervisor to force better performance?" Of the 204 respondents 20 percent replied yes and 68 percent answered no.

Responses to this questionnaire support the view that budgets are frequently perceived as acceptable by those who must live by them. Of course, 20 percent of these respondents did regard the budget quite negatively. Other research has revealed that budgets may also be viewed with fear and hostility. These reactions are most probable when the organization uses punishments and the threats of punishments to enforce its budgeting system.

CONTROLS AND CRISIS

Putting effective controls in place has a twofold benefit to crisis managers. First, such controls should diminish the likelihood or severity of crises. Second, these controls will serve as a basis for crisis assessment and evaluating the extent to which the crisis has been resolved.

Referring again to the classification matrix introduced in Chapter 3, it would be a fairly easy task to examine each cell, identify the various potential crisis in each cell, and recommend one or more control devices for each potential crisis. Moreover, it would be best to quantify each of these controls so that early warning signals can be quickly identified. This is not always an easy task, but well worth the effort.

CONCLUSION

Putting relevant controls in place is a critical element of crisis management, but one often overlooked. Employing the control process and specific controls identified in this chapter should facilitate this process greatly.

7

Understanding Your Stakeholders

Sooner or later we all quote our Mothers.

Bern Williams

GONE ARE THE DAYS

It's not like anyone was surprised. In January 2001, one of the longest ongoing retail establishments in the United States bit the dust. After more than 100 years in business, the Montgomery Wards department store chain filed for Chapter 11. It was a long time coming. Ever since the emergence of Wal-Mart in the 1960s, Ward's days were numbered.

Unlike their major competitors, such as Sears, JC Penny, and K-Mart, Montgomery Ward felt little need to remodel their stores, revamp product lines, or build stores in more upscale neighborhoods. Top management felt comfortable with their longstanding market niches, not fully comprehending that consumers in these markets were abandoning them. Moreover, many of these former customers were replaced with minorities, such as African Americans, Latinos, and immigrants from the Far East. Also, many of these new consumers had incomes too low to purchase traditional

Ward products. Moreover, most of these existing products had little appeal for these new market segments.

The decade of the 1990s saw a severe decline in customer visits, partly due to deteriorating customer service and incompetent sales personnel. The death knell proved to be Wards' inability to access modern technology, especially computer software capable of processing sales, controlling inventory, and managing trends. For example, there was no way Wards could participate in the Internet revolution.

A primary element of the crisis management process is the identification of those who create, and are affected by, crisis events. Once identified, there is a need to understand the possible reasons for their behavior. The information discussed in this chapter deals with the second area of concern.

Because there are so many labels placed on people, we employ the term "stakeholder." Stakeholders refers to the critical parties, including both individual people and institutions, who would be affected by a crisis or who could affect the organization's ability to manage a crisis. The trend in crisis management is to expand the list of stakeholders beyond the usual employees, managers, and unions to include customers and vendors. We suggest that effective crisis management requires an even greater expansion of relevant stakeholders to include parties even further removed from the organization, such as special-interest groups, local politicians, and even competitors.

Figure 7.1 focuses on the factors that influence human behavior, both external and internal. Obviously our discussion is quite limited and tends to concentrate on those factors particularly relevant to crisis management. The chapter concludes with an examination of those same factors, only in an organizational context.

Figure 7.1
Factors Influencing Stakeholder Decision Making

EXTERNAL INFLUENCES   INTERNAL INFLUENCES

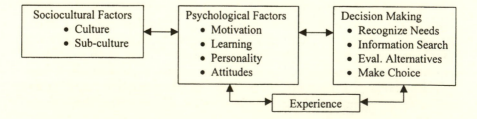

CULTURES

All of us are part of a cultural fabric that affects our behavior. Culture is the sum of learned beliefs, values, and customs that regulate the behavior of members of a particular society. Through our culture, we are taught how to adjust to the environmental, biological, psychological, and historical parts of our environment.

The three components of culture—beliefs, values, and customs— are each somewhat different. A belief is a proposition that reflects a person's particular knowledge and assessment of something (that is, "I believe that . . ."). Values are general statements that guide behavior and influence beliefs and attitudes. It has been stated that the function of a value system is to help a person choose between alternatives in everyday life. Values are formed at both the personal level and the cultural level. Values have both an importance and a judgment component. In family A, integrity is a very important value; in family B, it is not. In family A, integrity is equated with always standing up for one's beliefs, no matter what the consequences. In family B, integrity is equated with not cheating if there is a chance of getting caught. The formation of personal values is affected by cultural values and vice versa. Yet we retain many personal values despite contrary judgments by society. For example, the personal value of always finding humor in everything might not prove acceptable as you giggle through a professor's lecture. Customs are overt modes of behavior that constitute culturally approved ways of behaving in specific situations. For example, taking one's mother out for dinner and buying her presents on Mother's Day is an American custom that Hallmark and other card companies support enthusiastically. However, customs do vary from region to region and from country to country. Even families have their own set of customs. Beliefs and values are guides for behavior while customs are acceptable ways of behaving.

Values

Managers need to have a special interest in values, because values are influential in shaping behavior.

Dominant cultural values are referred to as core values; they tend to affect and reflect the core character of a particular society. For example, if a culture does not value efficiency but does value a sense of belonging and neighborliness, few people are likely to want to use automatic teller machines. Likewise, if a culture begins to value family and personal health and relaxation over achievement and material success, this cultural trend would be of interest to many businesses.

What do Americans value? To find out, Milton Rokeach originated the Rokeach Value Survey, which includes thirty-six value statements. The first eighteen reflect terminal values (that is, end results) and are designed to measure the relative importance of personal goals. The other eighteen statements reflect instrumental values and measure basic approaches an individual might follow to reach the terminal values. More recently, researchers assessed the applicability of Rokeach's thirty-six items and concluded that only twenty-four apply in a business setting. Other researchers have proposed the simplified List of Values (LOV), which consists of nine values: (1) a sense of belonging, (2) excitement, (3) fun and enjoyment in life, (4) warm relationships, (5) self-fulfillment, (6) being well respected, (7) a sense of accomplishment, (8) security, and (9) self-respect.

The publication *pr reporter* developed this list of global values:

The Six Value Segments

Altruists: slightly older, slightly more women than men

Strivers: more male, median age

Fun-seekers: more men than women, younger

Creatives: evenly split between men and women

Devouts: older, more women than men, anchored in religion, faith, tradition, security, health

Intimates: slightly more women than men, younger, focused on personal relationships

Generally, we move between groups as we age. In our teens, we're generally Fun-seekers. In our twenties, more are Creatives and Strivers. In our thirties and forties we become more concerned with personal relationships and move into the Intimates group. In our forties and fifties we move into the Altruist or Devout groups.

- Examples: Asia has a high number of Strivers; developed Asia, a large number of Fun-seekers; whereas developing Asia has more Devouts

A Closer Look at Values Segments

Devouts:

- Primary values: respect for ancestors, also protecting the family, honesty, faith, and duty. Neither faith nor duty are among global top ten
- Lowest weekly TV viewership and listenership of radio
- Lowest media involvement, excepting religious media
- High concentration of Devouts in Middle East, Africa, Indonesia, Saudi Arabia, India, and China

Altruists:
- Protecting family, honesty, and justice are among their primary values; justice not in global top ten
- Average overall media involvement
- High concentration in Latin America, Russia, Kazakhstan, Turkey, Spain, Argentina, Mexico, and Japan

Intimates:
- Primary values: family, honesty, stable personal relationships, friendship, and self-esteem
- Higher-than-average media involvement and they are most interested in media that can be shared with others, such as music and television
- High concentration in Judeo–Christian-based societies like Western Europe, Eastern Europe, the United States, and the United Kingdom (four in ten Britons are Intimates)

Strivers:
- Top values are family, material security, health and fitness, wealth, respecting ancestors
- Next to the Devout group, are the lowest users of media. They're too busy working for leisure time and social pursuit
- Print media are important to them
- Highest concentrations in Asia/Pacific, Hong Kong, Korea, China, Malaysia, and Thailand

Creatives:
- Most important values are honesty, freedom, authenticity, self-esteem, and learning
- Personal improvement is important to this group
- This is the group most engaged in media, especially print media, and personal computers
- Highest concentrations in Latin America, Western Europe, the United States, Chile, Australia, and Colombia

Fun-seekers:
- Key values are enjoying life, having fun, friendship, freedom, and protecting the family
- Heaviest users of video and recorded music, average overall media usage
- Highest concentrations of this group are in the developed world; that is, those with the economic ability to be fun seekers—Malaysia, Thailand, Japan, Germany, and Italy

Media Use

- Across cultures and values segments, consumers say they watch between 2½ and 3 hours of TV every day
- All groups describe the kind of shows they like as "interesting"
- Intimates average 2½ hours of radio every day
- Creatives are most interested in new media and books and are the most technologically advanced
- Newspapers are not an efficient way to reach Fun-seekers or Intimates, but Devouts and Creatives love newspapers

Concerns

- The number-one concern in the United States and worldwide is crime and lawlessness
- For Creatives, greatest concerns are environment and quality of education
- For Devouts, the greatest concern is government corruption

Some Characteristics

- Sports and leisure: While soccer is still the number-one sport in the world, basketball is quickly catching up—and is more gender balanced. Michael Jordan is the most recognizable person globally.
- Music: "MTV" generation is real. "Music transcends cultural, national, and even personal values of people worldwide." It's a universal language.
- Technology: People in the United States, France, and other places as diverse as Kazakhstan and Paraguay use new media (computers, WWW, etc.).

Three Intrinsic Factors Drive Global Markets

To understand people in a personal way, PR pros must take into account the following:

- Personal values
- Lifestage (where you are in your life, age-wise and lifestyle-wise)
- Nationality

SUBCULTURES

A natural evolution that occurs in any culture is the emergence of subcultures. Although the core values in a culture are held by virtually the entire population, secondary values are not. People who share a set of secondary values are referred to as a subculture. Examples include yuppies and environmentally concerned people.

Many factors can place an individual in one or several subcultures. According to one source, the most important are the following:

1. *Material culture.* The way in which benefits are distributed can create various subcultures. The poor, the affluent, and the white-collar middle class all stand out as examples of subcultures that have proven important to marketers.

2. *Social institutions.* By participating in social institutions such as marriage, parenthood, a retirement community, the army, and so on, a person may become part of a subculture.

3. *Belief systems.* These include religious and political affiliation. An individual's religious beliefs and their strength can influence habits, attitudes, values, and purchase patterns. For example, traditional Amish do not use several types of products, including electricity and automobiles. A whole set of factors has also been correlated with whether a person is a democrat, republican, independent, or socialist.

4. *Aesthetics.* Artistic people often form a subculture of their own associated with their common interest—including art, music, dance, drama, and folklore.

5. *Language.* Dialects, accents, and vocabulary can quickly place a person in a particular subculture. Southerners and northerners are two traditional categories.

Several caveats are necessary before we proceed. First, the sociocultural environment changes constantly. Ongoing monitoring is therefore necessary. The tendency for a company to think that it has the behaviors and values of a group figured out is probably the first indicator that the firm has stopped paying attention. This was clearly the case with thousands of businesses that decided that the consumer no longer cared about the environment. Second, there will be exceptions to every pattern or behavior. It is important to be prepared for these exceptions but not to assume that they negate the observed pattern. Third, as target markets get larger and businesses move into other countries, finding general patterns will become more difficult because each culture must be assessed separately.

THE PSYCHOLOGICAL BACKGROUND

Attempting to sell decorative outdoor lighting to a buyer in an industry plant who wants lighting solely for security purposes will probably get a salesperson nowhere. If sellers do not appeal to the right motive, they will probably lose the sale. Similarly, if a company misreads its stakeholders' beliefs, interest, attitudes, self-images, or other psychological characteristics, it risks making major mistakes. A company should learn as much as possible about the characteristics of it stakeholders.

Motivation

Much of what people do can be traced to their needs. An unsatisfied need causes an inner state of tension, feelings or disequilibrium, or dissatisfaction. A motive is an inner drive or pressure to take action in order to eliminate tension, to satisfy a need or solve a problem, or to restore a sense of equilibrium. Unstimulated, latent needs do not motivate behavior; a need must be aroused to a certain level in order for it to serve as a motive. The sources of arousal may be internal (biological or psychological) or environmental. Hunger, for example, may be aroused by a lack of food, by thoughts about food, or by a commercial for a tasty dish.

The most widely publicized theory of human motivation was developed by Abraham Maslow. His "hierarchy of human needs" theory postulates five basic levels of human needs, which rank in order of importance from low-level (biogenic) needs to higher-level (psychogenic) needs. The theory suggests that individuals seek to satisfy lower-level needs before higher-level needs. When a lower-level need is satisfied, a new, higher-level need emerges, and so on. If a lower-level need experiences some renewed depreciation, it may temporarily become dominant again.

Managers need to understand what motives stimulate what types of behavior and how these motives and behaviors are influenced by specific situations. Identifying potential motives would seem to be a first step in this task. At one time, conventional wisdom held that all motives are biologically based and innate, like hunger and thirst. But many motives are learned, primarily through socialization during early childhood. Motivations to achieve, to conform, to be powerful, to feel a sense of belonging all reflect the effects of learning. Since each individual's personal development is unique, so are each person's motives. Furthermore, even when behavior is motivated by biologically based needs learned motivations generally guide the expression of that behavior.

Because of the influence of learning, the number of possible motives for stakeholders' behavior is vast. There have been many attempts to classify these motives, but no one classification is complete or universally accepted. Probably the classification most closely associated with promotion divides motives into rational and emotional motives. Rational motives are supported by a systematic reasoning process that people perceive as being acceptable to their peers. A homemaker, for instance, might insist on buying foods grown without chemicals, even if they cost more than other foods, in order to enhance the family's health. Whether the arguments are valid or not is irrelevant; what matters is that the individual believes the motivation is rational. Rational motives for buying a product include lower price, greater endurance, higher quality, convenience, and better performance.

Learning

Learned motives are only one example of the pervasive influence of learning on human behavior. Some forms of learning, called cognitive learning, involve thought and conscious awareness; problem solving is an example. Behavior is changed through behavioral learning, which is learning that does not require awareness or conscious effort but depends instead on an association between events.

Although several theories attempt to explain how learning takes place, there are common principles and concepts that apply to all. Learning starts with motivation, which is based on needs and goals. Motivation thus acts as a spur to learning, with needs and goals serving as stimuli. Suppose a person is motivated to begin an exercise program because he is putting on weight and feeling lethargic. A cue—in this case, an ad for a new health club—provides the direction the individual will follow to satisfy the goal of losing weight. The message in this ad, however, will only serve as a cue if it is consistent with the person's expectations. If he has already failed to lose weight at other health clubs, this ad will not be a useful cue. How an individual reacts to a cue constitutes his or her response. Learning can take place even if the response is not overt. Several cues may be processed and evaluated before an individual finally reacts to one overtly. Response is a function of one's past experiences with cues. A positive response to a beneficial experience is called positive reinforcement; the cue is again likely to produce a similar reaction. If the experience was unpleasant, then negative reinforcement has taken place, and we will not repeat the same mistake again.

Attitudes

Motivation and learning both play a part in determining a third key component of the psychological background for human behavior: attitudes. An attitude is an enduring disposition, favorable or unfavorable, toward some object—an idea, a person, a thing, a situation. Thus attitudes toward brands are tendencies to evaluate brand in a consistently favorable or unfavorable way. Each attitude has three components: cognitive, affective, and behavioral. All three components must be consistent in order for a real attitude to result.

The cognitive component includes beliefs and knowledge about the object of the attitude. For example, an individual might believe that Shell Oil is a major manufacturer and aggressive marketer, and is quite profitable. Each of these beliefs reflects knowledge about an attribute of the company. All one's beliefs about Shell Oil represent the cognitive component of an attitude toward the company.

If someone says "I hate Shell Oil" or "I like the gasoline from Shell Oil better than any other," the person is expressing the affective aspect of an attitude. Feelings about the object make up the affective component of an attitude. People typically evaluate separately each attribute of the object of the attitude; the combination of these reactions determines the overall reaction. For example, a person might hold separate feelings about the products of a company, its honesty, its fairness toward its workers, and so forth.

Actions taken toward the object of an attitude constitute the behavioral component of the attitude. Buying a product, recommending a company to friends or requesting information are examples of behavioral components. Behavior is usually directed toward an entire object and is therefore not likely to be attribute specific. In the case of retail outlets, however, consumers may react behaviorally to specific attributes. For example, a homemaker may buy produce at one supermarket and meat at another.

How easily can attitudes be changed? The answer depends to an extent on two characteristics of the attitude: its centrality and its intensity.

Centrality depends on the degree to which an attitude is tied to values. Note that although personal values influence attitudes, the two are distinct. Values are not tied to a specific situation or object; they are standards that guide behavior and influence beliefs and attitudes. People have a large number of beliefs, a smaller number of attitudes, and even fewer values. The stronger the relationship between an attitude and a person's values, the greater the centrality of the attitude. For example, for a person who places a high value on thriftiness, social responsibility, and ecology, a favorable attitude toward recyclable containers is likely to have high centrality. If the centrality of an attitude is high, then changing it would create inconsistency between the attitude and a person's values. Not surprisingly, research suggests that the more central an attitude is, the more difficult it is to change.

Intensity depends on the affective component of an attitude. The strength of feeling toward the object of an attitude constitutes the intensity of the attitude. Intense attitudes are difficult to change. Consequently, most efforts are directed at creating minor changes in attitudes—from negative to neutral, from neutral to positive, or from positive to more positive. An individual who holds an intensely negative attitude toward a product or idea might best be eliminated from further consideration.

THE DECISION-MAKING PROCESS

Recognizing Needs and Problems

Earlier we discussed the difference between latent needs, which do not stimulate behavior, and unmet needs, which do motivate behavior. Another way of distinguishing between latent and unmet needs is to view the former as nonproblems and the latter as problems. For example, a recent college graduate may have a latent need for a new car to replace a 1986 pickup but takes no action. Within six months, the pickup requires a new battery and a brake job, and the garage has just called with a repair estimate for $374. The latent need has now been converted into an unmet need, or a problem to be solved.

Every day, people face a myriad of problems. Some are routine, such as filling the car with gasoline or buying milk. Other problems occur infrequently, such as searching for a good life insurance policy or a fiftieth anniversary gift. Whether the problem is routine or infrequent, the process of buying starts when an unsatisfied need creates tension and thus motivation. As discussed earlier, the motive may be aroused by internal sources or by external sources. Whether people recognize a need often depends on the type of information received and how it is perceived.

Even if people recognize a need, whether they act to resolve the problem depends on two factors: (1) the magnitude of the discrepancy between what they have and what they need, and (2) the importance of the problem. Every person has his or her own personal hierarchy of needs. This hierarchy varies from person to person, as well as across time and situations. For some people, having a cup of coffee the first thing every morning is a need with a very high priority. A consumer may want a new Mercedes and own a ten-year-old VW. Despite the large discrepancy between the current possession and the need, if the problem is relatively unimportant compared with other problems, the consumer is not likely to be motivated to buy the Mercedes. For buying to proceed, people must be motivated both to acknowledge the need and to do something about it.

Furthermore, the problem must be defined in such a way that the person can initiate action to bring about a solution. In many cases, problem recognition and problem definition occur simultaneously, as happens when a person runs out of toothpaste. But consider a more complicated problem that is involved with status and image—how we want others to see us. A person may know that she is not satisfied with her appearance; because she may not be able to define the problem more precisely she might not do anything about the situation.

Information Search and Processing

When a problem has been recognized, a state of tension occurs that causes the consumer to search for information that will help in decision making. The information search is the second step in decision making and involves mental as well as physical activity. The search takes time, energy, and money and can often require giving up more desirable activities. The benefits of the information search, however, often outweigh the costs. Engaging in a thorough information search may ultimately mean saving money, receiving better quality, or reducing risk.

The stakeholder becomes involved in two types of information search: internal and external. In an internal search, the person attempts to resolve problems by recalling previously stored information. For example, people who suffer from allergies can easily recall what they did last year for relief. They may even remember the location of the drugstore where they last purchased allergy medication. When problems cannot be resolved through an internal search, people search externally for additional information. The external sources may include family, friends, professionals, government or corporate publications, ads, sales personnel, or displays.

The sources that a person uses may depend on the importance of the decision, past experience, confidence in particular sources, and psychological makeup. Some people find it too troublesome to search for information and are willing to rely on the information provided by a salesclerk for a minor purchase. But when these same people buy a new car, they may go through a very elaborate search that includes writing for information, comparing government reports, driving from dealership to dealership, and talking with people who are considered knowledgeable about the product.

When the search actually occurs, what do people do with the information? How do they spot, understand, and recall information? In other words, how do they process information? This broad topic is important for understanding communication in general as well as buying behavior in particular, and it has received a great deal of study. Understanding the process people go through when they receive information has direct benefits for the crisis.

Steps in Information Processing

Assessing how a person processes information is not an easy task. Often observation has served as the bases. Yet, there are many theories as to how this process takes place. Figure 7.2 shows one widely accepted outline of the information-processing sequence.

Exposure

Information processing starts with the exposure of people to some source of stimulation such as watching television, going to the supermarket, or driving past a particular billboard. In order to start the process, a business must attract people to the stimulus or put it squarely in the path of people in the target market.

Attention

Exposure alone does little unless people pay attention to the stimulus. At any moment, people are bombarded by all sorts of stimulus but they have a limited capacity to process this input. They must devote mental resources to stimuli in order to process them; in other words, they must pay attention. If attention is not given, no further information processing occurs, and the message will be lost.

Attention is selective. We have neither the cognitive capability nor the interest to pay attention to all the messages we are exposed to. Some stimuli are more attention-getting than others. For example, bright colors and movement both attract attention. Contrast (that is, size of the stimulus reactive to its background) and intensity (for example, loudness, brightness) also prompt attention. People are likely to pay attention to a message when it provides information that is relevant to problems that evoke high involvement and that they are motivated to resolve. People also tend to pay attention to messages that are perceived to be consistent with their attitudes and ignore those perceived not to be in agreement.

Figure 7.2
The Five Steps in Information Processing

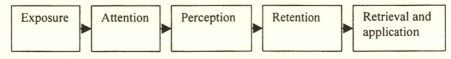

Perception

Step three in the information-processing sequence is perception. It involves classifying the incoming signals into meaningful categories, forming patterns, and assigning names or images to them. Perception is the assignment of meaning to stimuli received through the senses.

CASE 7: AT AN ALL-TIME LOW

Jackson Community College has been in existence for nearly forty years and has an excellent reputation for high quality programs and feeding the four-year colleges in the region with well-prepared students. Many of the JCC faculty have been employed there for twenty years or more and are very proud of this affiliation.

While faculty salaries and supportive resources have never been great, what began in the spring of 1998 quickly made the situation at JCC deplorable. It was then that the state legislative voted an 11-percent decrease in the capital allocation to all the junior colleges in the state. The rumor mill was immediate. Faculty were led to believe that 10 percent would be fired and those that remained would take a 5-percent salary cut. Likewise, staff would be greatly reduced, along with a salary reduction. Plans to replace equipment at JCC were, supposedly, cancelled. In fact, none of these rumors were true—or not immediately so. Nonetheless, the morale at JCC was extremely bad and many faculty were considering other job alternatives.

Observation

The rumor mill is a fact of life in most organizations, and a possible source of crisis. Managing it is a serious challenge. Perception is everything, and if the faculty and staff believe that there is a danger of their being fired, they will leave. Then a true crisis will occur on the campus.

Perceptions are shaped by (1) the physical characteristics of the stimuli, (2) the context, and (3) the individual perceiving the stimuli. The senses transmit signals about the shape, color, sound, and feel of stimuli, but every individual perceives those stimuli within a particular context shaped by a person's own frame of reference. Thus a person's past learning, attitude, personality, self-image, and current motivations and emotions shape which is perceived. Some stimuli are perceived totally, some partially, some accurately, some inaccurately. In any event, the result of the perceptual process is a highly personalized mental representation of sensory stimuli representation that differs from person to person.

An individual interprets stimuli according to a set of prescribed criteria. Although this interpretation can be affected by many factors, there are a few general factors that appear to always operate. Clarity of the stimulus is critical; stimuli that are ambiguous or fuzzy run the risk of being misperceived. A person's past experience also influences interpretation. Prejudice, either racial or some other type, is simply taking certain stimuli and generalizing from our experience, whether accurate or inaccurate. Our motives and interests also influence interpretation. We tend to interpret clearly when we are interested in the topic.

Comprehension is part of the perceptual process, but it goes beyond labeling and identification to produce a more thorough evaluation of the perceived stimuli. Our first exposure to a red bicycle simply provides the perceptual reaction: "This is a red bike." A split second later we add to that assessment through comprehension: "Red bikes are best" or "Red bikes are ugly." In general, people comprehend messages in a way that makes them consistent with preexisting attitudes and opinions. People who believe that American-made automobiles are best therefore tend to discount or distort perceptions that challenge this view.

Retention

Storage of information for later reference, or retention, is the fourth step of the information-processing sequence. Actually, the role of memory in the sequence is twofold. First, memory holds information while it is being processed throughout the sequence. For example, in order for a stimulus to be perceived at all, it must first be held for an extremely brief time in what psychologists call sensory memory. Second, memory stores information for future, long-term use.

Memory itself is a process involving several stages. First is encoding: Before a person can remember anything, it must be put into a form the memory system can use. If a person reads a paragraph, for example, she might encode the general meaning of the passage, the image of the primary words, or the sound of the words. Once encoded, information can be stored in memory.

Information can be encoded and stored automatically, without constant effort. But rehearsal, the mental repetition of material, is often necessary to ensure that these processes occur. Rote repetition is sometimes sufficient but it is not as effective as elaborative rehearsal, which involves thinking about the information and relating it to other, already stored information. A person might remember a name if he or she simply repeats it to himself or herself, but he or she is more likely to remember it if he or she also thinks about the name and associates it with something else.

Retrieval and Application

The process by which information is recovered from the memory storehouse is called retrieval. Combined with application, retrieval represents the final stage in information processing. Its consumer can retrieve relevant information about a product or brand store, then he or she will apply it to solve a problem or meet a need.

Research findings suggest that the most effective way for marketers to facilitate retrieval of product information is to provide information and the product's benefits and attributes and then ensure a strong connection between them. This association between attributes and benefits is closely illustrated in the cereal industry, which presents the key attribute of fiber as a means of achieving the benefit of cancer prevention. Auto companies that include air bags as standard safety equipment provide a similar connection between the attribute and the benefit—in this case, prevention of serious injury in a car crash.

Identifying and Evaluating Alternatives

Once a need is recognized and defined and the information search is completed, alternatives are identified and evaluated. How people search for alternatives depends in part on such factors as (1) the cost in time and money, (2) how much information they already have, (3) the perceived risk associated with a wrong decision, and (4) their predispositions about making choices. That is, some people find the process of looking at alternatives to be difficult and disturbing. As a result, they tend to keep the number of alternatives to a minimum, even if they do not have enough information to determine that they are looking at their best options. Other people feel compelled to collect a long list of alternatives, a tendency that can slow down decision making.

Selection Behavior

After searching and evaluating, at some point people have to decide whether they are going to act. Anything we can do to simplify decision making will be attractive to people because most people find it hard to make a decision. Perhaps marketers can suggest in their advertising the best size of a product for a particular food. Sometimes several decision situations can be combined and marketed as one package. For example, travel agents often package travel tours, combining airfare, ground transportation, and hotels.

To do a better job at this stage of the decision-making process, a stakeholder needs to know answers to many questions about behavior. For many purchase decisions, the salesperson is the key. This is particularly true for industrial products and retail sales. In recent years, direct marketers have played a prominent role in reshaping the purchasing process of millions of consumers. Because of time constraints and the risks associated with traditional purchasing mechanisms, direct marketers have responded with better products, improved service, and reduced risks through warranties and guarantees. These benefits are highlighted in promotional messages produced by direct marketers.

A person's feelings and evaluations after the decision are also significant to a business because they can influence repeat behavior and what the stakeholder tells others.

Stakeholders typically experience some post-purchase anxiety after all but routine and low-risk decisions. This anxiety reflects a phenomenon called cognitive dissonance. According to this theory, people strive for consistency among their cognitions (knowledge, attitudes, beliefs, values). When there are inconsistencies, dissonance exists that people will try to eliminate. In some cases, the person makes the decision already aware of dissonant elements. In other instances, dissonance is aroused by disturbing information received after the choice.

To avoid or eliminate dissonance, people may avoid negative information. They may change their behavior, their opinions, or their attitudes. They may seek information or opinions that support their choice. Sometimes the person's attempt to reduce dissonance can produce dire consequences for the business. For example, in the process of convincing oneself that the purchase of a new GE microwave oven was a good decision, the consumer seeks additional information from friends. Unfortunately, the consumer's best friend says she had a terrible experience with her GE microwave oven.

The business may take specific steps to reduce post-purchase dissonance. Advertising that stresses the many positive attributes or confirms the popularity of the product can be helpful. Providing personalized reinforcement has proven effective with big-ticket items such as automobiles and major appliances. Salespeople in these areas may send cards or publicity materials or may even make personal calls in order to reassure customers about their purchase.

ORGANIZATIONAL MARKET BEHAVIOR

Those who supply goods and services to consumer markets are themselves in need of goods and services to run their businesses. These organizations—producers, resellers, and governments—make up vast organizational markets that buy a large variety of products, including equipment, raw materials, labor, and other services. Some organizations sell exclusively to other organizations and never come in contact with consumer buyers.

Despite the importance of organizational markets, far less research has been conducted on factors that influence their behavior than on factors that influence consumers. However, we can identify characteristics that distinguish organizational buying from consumer buying and typical steps in the organizational buying process.

Characteristics of Organizational Buying

Many elements of the sociocultural environment discussed in the previous sections influence organizational as well as consumer buying, but some additional forces are salient only in the organization setting. In particular, each organization has its own business philosophy that guides its actions in resolving conflicts, handling uncertainty and risk, searching for solutions, and adapting to change. For example, Peabody Coal, which is part of a declining industry, relies on a conservative purchase strategy in an attempt to maintain the status quo.

Five characteristics mark the organizational buying process:

1. In organizations, many individuals are involved in making buying decisions.
2. The organizational buyer is motivated by both rational and emotional factors in choosing products and services. Although the use of rational and quantitative criteria dominate in most organizational decisions, the decision makers are people, subject to many of the same emotional criteria used in personal purchases.
3. Organizational buying decisions frequently involve a range of complex technical dimensions. A purchasing agent for Volvo Automobiles, for example, must consider a number of technical factors before ordering a radio to go into the 240DL model. The electronic system, the acoustics of the interior, and the shape of the dashboard are a few of these considerations.
4. The organizational decision process frequently spans a considerable time, creating a significant lag between the marketer's initial contact

with the customer and the purchasing decision. Since many new factors can enter the picture during this lag time, the marketer's ability to monitor and adjust to these changes is critical.

5. Organizations cannot be grouped into precise categories. Each organization has a characteristic way of functioning and a personality.

The first item in this list of characteristics has important implications. Unlike the consumer buying process, organizational buying involves decision making by groups and enforced rules for making decisions. These two characteristics greatly complicate the task of understanding the buying process. For example, to predict the behavior of an organization with certainty, it is important to know who will take part in the decision process, what criteria each member uses in evaluating prospective suppliers, and what influence each member has. It is also necessary to understand something not only about the psychology of the individuals involved but also how they work as a group.

Who makes the decision to buy depends in part on the situation. Three types of buying situations have been distinguished: the straight re-buy, the modified re-buy, and the new task. The straight re-buy is the simplest situation: The company reorders a good or service without any modifications. The transaction tends to be routine and may be handled totally by the purchasing department. With the modified re-buy, the buyer is seeking to modify product specifications, prices, and so on. The purchaser is interested in negotiation, and several participants may take part in the buying decision. A company faces a new task when it considers buying a product for the first time. The number of participants and the amount of information sought tend to increase with the cost and risks associated with the transaction. This situation represents the best opportunity for the business.

CONCLUSION

Knowing as much as possible about the stakeholders that impact their world gives the crisis manager important advantages. Fundamental questions about the creation of harmful events as well as potential responses can be addressed. This chapter provided an overview of human behavior germane to crisis management. Much more must be learned relative to specific events.

8

Triggering Events

Even if you're on the right track, you'll get run over if you just sit there.

Will Rogers

ONE SMALL MISTAKE

For a company that's in the business of tracking customer satisfaction, it wasn't at all satisfying in a recent case. A press release issued by California-based J. D. Power & Company contained a single typographical error that turned out to be anything but minor. In fact, it cost the privately owned marketing-research firm some measure of its reputation and $200,000. The mistake concerned the service satisfaction reported by customers of U.S. West, the Denver-based Baby Bell. Instead of the reported "92" score and the dubious ranking of "dead last" among the Bells, the company actually garnered a "94"—and a more palatable tie with Ameritech and Southwestern Bell. The efficiency of today's media being what it is, the incorrect information was carried far and wide, most often in a context unflattering to U.S. West. Of course, companies complain all the time about J. D. Power surveys. Companies such as Florida Power & Light criticized its average ranking by the firm as not consistent with its in-house polls.

After all our planning for a crisis or triggering event, it has finally happened. Will all our hard work pay off? Will irrational behavior supercede the rational process we outlined? Will dominant personalities destroy our proactive organization?

Essentially, four basic decisions must be addressed. How should we identify triggering events? Does this event warrant a solution? How quickly should it be resolved? What elements of our crisis management plan need to be implemented in order to resolve the crisis?

In the rest of this chapter, we attempt to answer these questions. Before we begin this discussion, however, we examine the decision to pretest our crisis plan.

TESTING THE CRISIS PLAN

After the crisis plan is developed, you need to test it to ensure you have all the bases covered. We recommend doing at least one dry run to determine whether the plan has any unforeseen glitches. The extent of this plan is somewhat dependent on the size of the organization. Still, even a small business can focus their test on one or two of their most inevitable crises.

Only a few select people should know when the test will occur, and what the crisis will be to ensure a valid test. The test procedure will need to be thoroughly prepared to guarantee it doesn't disrupt business or create false rumors about your company because someone finds out about it and believes it to be a true crisis.

The test should be a mock crisis situation that could actually occur in real life. Depending upon your situation, you may want to try one of the scenarios you originally discussed when developing the plan, or you may want to make up something entirely different. If you are using a scenario that the team previously discussed, it is best to add some twists and turns that they would not be anticipating, to see how well the team is able to respond. For example, throw in a few protestors or angry customers that somehow make it through your front-line personnel and manage to reach someone who is not on the crisis team. Or, have a fake reporter interviewing employees as they leave the workplace at the end of the day.

Again, we cannot emphasize enough that planning this testing process thoroughly is critical. Don't let the test become a crisis.

CASE 8: LIES, LIES?

Fear is a sales pitch that has been used for decades to flog everything from alarm systems to underarm deodorant. But just think how it can be used on the Internet to whip up paranoia.

A little Toronto-based outfit called Bio Business International has already become quite adept at spreading myths through its Web site. Bio Business markets only one product—100-percent cotton, nonchlorine bleached tampons under the brand name Terra Femme. Among other things, the site encourages women to spread a terrifying message that tampons made by U.S. competitors may be horribly dangerous.

Specifically, the site warns that tampons made with rayon or that contain dioxin—a byproduct of some bleaching process—can be harmful. "Dioxin is now PROVEN to cause many kinds of cancer in women and men, along with birth defects, and to disrupt the natural hormones in our bodies," the Terra Femme site says.

Bio Business also invokes repeatedly the horror of toxic shock syndrome, a potentially fatal bacterial infection. The claim: 100-percent cotton tampons are safer than rayon or rayon blends when it comes to protecting women from toxic shock.

Observations

With millions of Web sites, it may be impossible for a company to monitor all inflammatory messages.

Identifying Triggering Events

Recall the crises continuum that was introduced in Chapter 1. Clearly, the triggering events on the right side of the continuum, that is, catastrophes, are fairly easy to identify; people are hurt, property is destroyed, companies close. However, the further we move to the left on the continuum, the more difficult it is to identify triggering events. A minor incident, such as a protest group marching in front of one of your branch stores for a few hours is unlikely to reach the attention of top management. Still, the premise of this book is that every crisis, no matter how trivial, is worth noting. As indicated in the section to follow, it doesn't mean that every crisis event is worth solving.

In order to identify all possible triggering events it is necessary to initiate the guidelines provided in Chapters 2 through 7. It would begin with putting a viable research plan in place. As noted in Chapter 2, this would include establishing a research net that would collect all relevant secondary information. This would include company records and intelligence, previous company research, trade or association studies, census data, libraries and universities, the Internet, and measures of reported and actual behavior. For example, Aspen Country Hardware has noted in several Web sites that there are many new competitors who offer consumers home repair advice and access to tools and materials. They also checked their sales records and determined that sales are off 12 percent compared to the same time last year. Several hardware trade publications had feature stories focusing on the increased popularity of online hardware sales. This trend was a clear triggering event for Aspen Hardware, gained through secondary information.

Primary research can also be used to identify triggering events. This original research can take the form of mail or personal interviews, focus groups, observations, and so forth. Aspen Country Hardware decided to conduct a short mail survey to confirm that the drop in sales was because of a shift to Internet purchases. They developed a ten-question survey and mailed it to a database of customers. The results indicated that, indeed, many of their customers had shifted their purchases to the Internet. However, they also included an open-ended question asking customers for complaints and suggestions. The answers to this question identified several other possible triggering events. For instance, several customers noted that the planned highways realignment in front of the store will mean that customers will have to cross two lanes of traffic to access the store. Also, five people indicated that they expected Aspen Country Hardware to create a Web site. Finally, thirty-seven customers suggested that they no longer shop at Aspen Country Hardware because their prices are too high and selection limited.

Ultimately, research had identified several crises to which Aspen Country Hardware is vulnerable. These actual crises can be categorized as follows:

- New competition via technology
- Product prices
- Traffic denies access
- Product selection
- Web site availability

Referring to the process provided in Chapter 3, a company can identify other potential crises. For our example, Aspen Country

Hardware conducted several meetings with employees and a focus group with ten customers. They identified other potential crises:

• Employee layoffs due to declining sales
• Retirement of primary owner
• Limited suppliers of lumber
• New ACE Hardware being built one-half mile away
• Lawsuit pending with customer who fell in store
• Declining financial performance
• Store built on flood plain

This list of twelve potential and actual crises are further tempered by the goals related to crisis management (Chapter 4). Recall that crises-related goals are unique in several ways:

1. Be both proactive and reactive
2. Considered in terms of the entire organization
3. Begin with top management
4. Must reflect corporate needs and values

Although Aspen Country Hardware does not have an explicit set of crises-related goals, the Christian values of both owners suggest that two goals are relevant:

1. Aspen Country Hardware will not go into debt
2. Employees always come first

Since Aspen Country Hardware cannot afford to build a Web site, that particular crisis may go unattended. Likewise, the layoff of employees will occur only if the business fails.

The list of crises or triggering events can change because of the company's organizational structure. Essentially, this implies that there must be organizational elements that account for crises management. This requires a contingency approach to organization and an organization that can directly address actual and potential crisis. Aspen Country Hardware employs a manager, two assistant managers, six full-time employees and eight part-time employees, plus the two owners. The City of Aspen has a population of 12,500 and is gradually losing population due to their location and limited job opportunities. Consequently, the Aspen Country Hardware organization has little flexibility. The partners agree, however, that they must establish an organization structure that can manage current and potential crisis. A four-person committee was established, made up of one owner, the manager, one assistant manager, and one full-time employee. The committee meets bi-weekly and on an as-needed basis.

Degree of control is an important classification criteria when evaluating crises. Anything a company can do to increase control is warranted. As explained in Chapter 6, there are specific control mechanisms that are possible. Having them in place can also influence the salience of the crisis events listed. Examples include financial standard, training, sales, and costs. Aspen Country Hardware has established controls that help them plan for crises. All employees are expected to have twenty-five hours of training each year. Cost controls are also in place, as are specific rewards for employees that reach stated sales goals.

In Chapter 7, we discussed the reasons why we need to understand as much as possible about our stakeholders. Culture, subculture, personal characteristics, and behavioral factors all must be considered. While no actual consumer research was conducted by the management of Aspen Country Hardware, employees all live in the community and are quite familiar with the local culture. How store-loyal are the local residents? Is their use of new technology a permanent change in behavior or a fad? Will vendors remain loyal?

We now have all the elements in place to identify most crisis-triggering events. To illustrate, let's examine the twelve actual and potential crises faced by Aspen Country Hardware in light of the variables just discussed.

List of Actual/Potential Crises	Influencing Factors
New competition via technology	Structure, control, stakeholders
Product prices	Goals, control, stakeholders
Traffic denies access	Structure, stakeholders
Product selection	Structure, control, stakeholders
Web site availability	Goals, stakeholders
Employee layoffs due to declining sales	Goals, structure, control
Retirement of primary owner(s)	Structure, control
Limited suppliers of lumber	Structure, control
New ACE Hardware being built one-half mile away	Structure, control, stakeholders
Pending lawsuit	Goals, control
Declining financial performance	Goals, structure, control
Store built on flood plain	Structure

The Initial Response

For every crisis on the event continuum, an initial-response decision must be made. That is, the organization must determine whether they choose to respond to the triggering event, or simply disregard it. This latter alternative may seem contrary to the proactive perspective exposed in this book, but ignoring a disruptive event is sometimes the best response.

Once again we refer to the crisis classification matrix (Figure 3.2) as a basis for our discussion. Recall that we employed four criteria; time pressure, degree of control, response options, and threat level. Moreover, the higher the number assigned to each box in the matrix, the more serious the crisis. We suggest that four criteria for assessment be considered when considering your initial response:

1. Identify the perceived importance of the problem area as indicated. The cell numbers in the classification matrix are initial indicators of importance. It is highly unlikely that a company should ever disregard an event that threatens human health or life. Still, these importance or seriousness scores are not absolute. For instance, one or two customer complaints may seem unimportant. Hundreds or thousands of complaints is a whole other story. This is a case where minor events can turn into major catastrophes. It may be necessary to conduct consumer research to accurately assess the perceived importance of the event.

2. Assess the size of discrepancy between the existing and expected states of nature. This same research will help you address this second criteria. Take for example an event like sexual harassment. There are some people who have a zero tolerance for sexual harassment; that is, one incident is too many. There are also people who feel that sexual harassment is inevitable in some businesses and unless these events are running rampant, they are best ignored. Similarly, in some parts of the world, small oil spills are daily occurrence and locals would not expect the guilty company to take action. This would hardly be true if an oil spill occurred off the coast of California. Obviously, when we suggest doing research, it cannot be done after the event has happened. Such research should be an ongoing process and all potential negative events should be considered. For those who have neither the expertise nor the resources to conduct such research, refer back to Chapter 2 for simple, cost-effective research techniques.

3. What is the level of response uncertainty? This question will be somewhat addressed in a later chapter when we highlight the efforts of the tobacco industry to reconcile with the general public, especially smokers. Although most would agree that the industry should make every effort to make up for their sins, few would agree that it will matter.

Again, very targeted research should be considered. Likewise, past experience with similar events or the experiences of other companies might provide important insights. In any case, there may be a very thin line between taking no action, because research shows that no apology will be accepted, and making some corrective response, if for no other reason than the morale of your employees.

4. What are the perceived negative consequences if the problem is disregarded? In this instance, all the stakeholders influenced by this decision should be considered. How will employees perceive you if you disregard the event? Government agencies? The general public? Competition? And, perhaps most important, how will this decision impact your existing business strategy? If you have positioned yourself as a benevolent company, does this position change as a result of this decision? If you are known for your high production standards, are they reduced because you chose to disregard complaints from a handful of customers? If a local restaurant decides not to remodel after a small fire, does the perception of the owners caring about the comfort of its customers lessen?

Immediate or Delayed?

One of the major differences in the approach used in this book compared to other books on crisis management is the attitude toward response time. Because virtually all the traditional examples of crisis would fall under the catastrophe category, the general recommendation is "speed is of the essence." People's lives may be at stake, so quick response time is critical.

While this is still true for the very serious crisis events, a delayed response may be more appropriate for many lesser crisis. Observe that one of the classification criteria employed in Figure 3.2 is time pressure. Therefore, a starting point in assessing response time is to consider the types of events found under the "intense" column compared to those listed under the "minimal" column. Further, events lower in the column represent the quickest response time (see boxes 11, 12, 15, 16). Conversely, those under the "minimal" column may justify a delayed response.

Two other points of clarification are necessary. First, determining what "immediate" and "delayed" mean must be resolved. In even the most serious catastrophes, "immediate" does not necessarily mean minutes after the event. Even in the case of a plane crash it takes several minutes to gather the necessary information, check the facts, and follow prescribed protocols, such as not releasing the names of the victims. Consequently, an immediate response may have time stages, corresponding to the nature of the event. A delayed response, such as responding to a customer complaint, may also be resolved through stages. An unhappy customer may receive a call or note from the manager the next day and a more formal letter of apology or inquiry a few days later. It is recommended that each potential crisis event have a response-time definition as part of the crisis plan.

A second question related to response time is examining whether different response personnel are operating under a different response time. Any of the following departments may have crisis communication responsibilities in a given organization: legal, financial, operations, security, public affairs and public relations, health and safety, and human relations. It is conceivable, based on the nature of the event, that operations must make an immediate response, while legal and public relations have more time to respond. Again, all the information should be delineated in the crisis plan.

The Crisis Response Process

Our crisis plan is in place. This includes an understanding of the stated objectives, a recognition of all the relevant stakeholders, an installation of the necessary controls that help prevent crisis as well as monitor potential crisis, and an organization structure that is crisis responsive and is able to accommodate the many possible contingencies.

Although there are several control mechanisms now installed that should alert the organization of all impending crisis events, there are several general warning signals that suggest a possible triggering event. The first is referred to as "management by exception." That is, a serious discrepancy between actual and expected performance is noted. Sales or returns represent two common examples. The second warning signal may come from employee observations. An assembly line employee might observe an improper installation of a guidance system, or an employee at a restaurant notes that the temperature in the freezer is too low. Customers are always a good source of problems. Because customers are unlikely to report problems unless they are serious or directly affect them, an organization is wise in establishing a mechanism that encourages customer input. This can be done at the point of sale, a suggestion box, a Web site, or through a regular customer survey. The final source of crisis-related information are reports on relevant industries. As this book goes to press, the entire high-technology industry is under severe crisis. Thousands of employees are being dismissed, plants are closing, and all this is creating a domino effect that has impacted the world economy. What will happen to the traditional publishing industry if on-line publishing catches on?

Since every organization has its own unique crisis response plan, it is impossible to provide a standardized example. However, we do suggest that closely following the recommendations provided in Chapters 1 through 7 will facilitate the creation of your own unique plan. Moreover, dealing with crisis appears to be a two-stage process in most instances: (1) resolve the actual crisis event, and (2) communicate with the necessary stakeholders about the crisis event. The second element may be as important as the first in many cases. As such, the next three chapters all deal with communication.

9

Human Communications

> Real communication happens when people feel safe.
> Ken Blanchard, *The Heart of a Leader*

TOO MUCH, TOO LATE

Philip Morris Companies lit a fire when it turned corporate philanthropy into a $100-million ad campaign that presented its Philip Morris, USA, Kraft Foods, and Miller Brewing Company subsidiaries as good corporate citizens. The image was introduced in October 1999, accompanied by a new Web site, www.philipmorris.com, acknowledging that "there is no 'safe' cigarette and that cigarette smoking is addictive, as that term is most commonly used today."

Philip Morris combined the good deeds and tobacco messages because both are part of a "broad effort to define ourselves" say spokesperson Peggy Roberts. "We haven't been open about a lot, and we're putting all the information in one place [on the Web site]. Some of it we've said before. It's not all as new as people characterize it to be."

President Clinton was among those criticizing the admission. For businesses, the question is whether the communication blitz will prompt consumer backlash against Philip Morris.

Philip Morris also keeps its top executives on the road speaking to parent–teacher organizations, civic groups, hospital associations, and nonprofit partners about the company's charitable programs.

Themed "Working to make a difference. The people of Philip Morris," TV spots dramatize true stories from Philip Morris's work in hunger, disaster relief, domestic violence, and curbing youth access to tobacco. One spot shows how Kraft helps food banks deliver fresh produce; another recounts how Miller bottled drinking water rather than beer in an Alabama plant to help flood victims.

The $100-million communication strategy employed by Philip Morris companies has been criticized by many. Can Philip Morris ever repair decades of bad deeds that they're now admitting? Can they ever win consumers' trust, or even get it to neutral? Would they be better off spending this money at the local level, creating a grassroots support system? Is throwing more and more money at this problem ever going to pay off?

Historically, crisis communication has received the majority of the time and efforts of crises managers, or more likely, the public relations agency responsible for crisis-related communications. Fundamental questions include the following: Do we respond? When? To who? Who is our spokesperson? What is said? Training is provided in media relations, public speaking, emergency response tactics, interpersonal skills, and so forth. A separate industry has evolved around crisis communication.

A great deal of excellent information can be garnered from existing crisis communication strategy, and much of it will be reviewed in the next chapter. However, we feel that a review of basis communication thought and principles is a helpful foundation for effective crisis management.

Crisis management includes a basic understanding of human communication and, more specifically, of communication that attempts to persuade. This chapter describes how communication takes place and which components of the process can be manipulated in order to enhance persuasiveness.

As discussed earlier, understanding people is a prerequisite for effective persuasive communication. We begin by taking an overview of the context in which crisis management occurs. That context is known as business communication.

BASIC FEATURES OF BUSINESS COMMUNICATION

The role of business communication is to support the business plan and help key audiences understand and believe in the company's advantage over the competition. As Figure 9.1 illustrates, business communication has an external and an internal flow.

Figure 9.1
The Flow of Business Communication

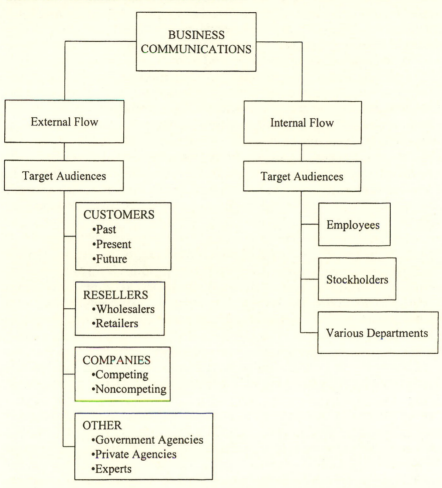

The external flow is directed at past, present, and potential customers; at resellers, both wholesalers and retailers; at other companies; and at various audiences, such as government agencies, private agencies, and experts in the field. A large, multinational company such as Polaroid, for example, maintains an elaborate network of external communications. It communicates with past customers through advertising and direct mail; with current customers through advertising, warranties, product updates, and material on how to use its products; and with potential customers through advertising, point-of-purchase displays, salespeople, and so on. Through direct mail and its sales force, Polaroid also communicates information about its products, pricing, and promotion to resellers. It exchanges similar information with competitors and with companies that sell complementary products such as photo albums. Finally, Polaroid keeps government agencies (such as the Federal Trade Commission) and consumer interest groups (for example, photography clubs) informed about its efforts.

The internal flow of communication involves employees in general, specific departments of the organization, and stockholders. Employees often need to know what the company is doing, especially when the organization is introducing new products or deleting old ones, changing prices, or distributing the product in new outlets or markets. By influencing how employees perceive their organization, communication can help shape their morale and performance. If employees feel they are working for an innovative market leader that produces highly regarded outputs, for example, they are likely to work harder, stay with the company longer, and become positive opinion leaders in public. Departments must communicate with all the other areas of the firm. Research and engineering departments, for example, share product information with marketing, and vice versa. Through sales forecasts, marketing determines the day-to-day level of production. Stockholders also need to be informed about activities. If they are going to buy stock and recommend the company to other buyers, they must be convinced that business decisions are in their interest.

A business also communicates with members of the firm in different locations. Making sure that employees in different cities and regions receive the same messages and understand them in a similar way is critical for the cohesion of the organization as well as for the coordinated implementation of the business strategy. Of course, this task becomes even more difficult when a company must communicate internationally. On an international level, the flow of vital intrafirm information can easily be distorted by factors such as cultural differences and physical distance.

Whether the flow is internal or external, effective communication means reaching the right people with the right information through the right sources at the right time. It requires an integrated strategy, which should do the following:

1. Assess the relative importance that members of the audience place on specific categories of information. Do they want objective information, replete with facts and comparisons? Or do they desire emotional appeals, which prompt them to act? What do they already know?
2. Select communication vehicles that are most effective in delivering information. Which vehicles does the audience use regularly? Which

are trusted most? Does the audience turn to different vehicles for some purposes, such as an expensive purchase?

3. Gauge where the communicator stands in relation to competing sources. Is the audience committed to a particular source, such as friends or *Consumer Reports* magazine? Is the audience open to new sources? What are they?

4. Provide guidelines to determine what mix of communication techniques to use and how best to allocate funds. These guidelines should be based on the communication objectives, available resources, and so forth.

Implementing a strategy requires a thorough understanding of the needs and wants of the various audiences, a working knowledge of the available communication techniques and how they blend together, and an awareness of competing communicators, including other companies, friends, the government, the news media, and so forth. In short, a great deal of data must be gathered before the business can implement a communication strategy.

The crisis strategy is part of this overall communication effort by a business. Crisis management is concerned with communication intended to inform and persuade. If executives and business owners understand communication, they should be better able to manage the crisis. In the next section of this chapter, we discuss basic ideas about how people communicate and present some key ideas to effective communication.

THE HUMAN COMMUNICATION SYSTEM

The study of communication has a long and varied tradition in Western culture. The scholars of classical Greece and Rome studied communication (or rhetoric) intensively; since that time, the process of how one person communicates with others has been a topic of fascination.

What is meant by communication? The word communication is derived from the Latin *communis*, meaning "common." To communicate is to use symbols to share some idea, attitude, or information so that meaning is held in common. Scholars through the ages have tried to formulate more precise definitions. Communication has a beginning, middle, and ending and is guided by the communication objectives of the participants. Beyond this point of agreement, two definitional perspectives are popular today.

The first perspective assumes that for something to be communication, the person producing the message must intend to influence someone's behavior through a symbolic message. Critics of this perspective argue that this view ignores apparently subconscious attempts to communicate feelings or fears. Those who favor the intentional approach answer that intent can be either conscious or unconscious. Thus, an ad for Perrier water communicates directly through the words and music contained in the ad. The ad also communicates at the unconscious level through the use of certain types of actors, their outfits, and the location of the commercial.

According to the second perspective, communication does not require an intent to influence. Rather, this perspective holds that everything we do or say and every event around us is communication if someone perceives meaning in it. This means that if someone assigns meaning to a behavior or an event, then communication has occurred, whether or not anyone engaged in an intentional act. Thus, simply for another person to perceive meaning in a stimulus makes a behavior communication.

Both of these perspectives contain some truth. In this book, we encompass both points of view by defining human communication as a process in which two or more persons attempt to consciously or unconsciously influence each other through the use of symbols.

THE PROCESS OF COMMUNICATION

Figure 9.2 illustrates the basic elements of the process of human communication. Note, however, that these elements are all closely related. In fact, even something as complex as communication within a large factory can be viewed as a single entity, with components and interrelationships within it. If one element is changed, each of the others is altered. In other words, speakers, messages, and listeners together form a system. Still, in order to understand the system, we need to discuss each component separately.

First, consider the communicators, a component of every communication system. In the traditional communication model, the two communicators are referred to as the sender (encoder) and the receiver (decoder). The source, or initiator, of the communication process can be an individual, a group, or an institution that wishes to transmit a message to the receiver, which may be another individual, group, or institution. The sender accomplishes the transmission of the message by selecting and combining a set of symbols in order to convey some meaning to the receiver. The greater the similarity or overlap between the sender and receiver, the more likely that communication will be effective and the less likely that miscommunication will take place. Therefore, if the overlap is not natural, it behooves the sender to learn as much about the receiver as possible. Successful salespeople, for example, are adept at qualifying a prospective customer.

Figure 9.2
A Model of Human Communication

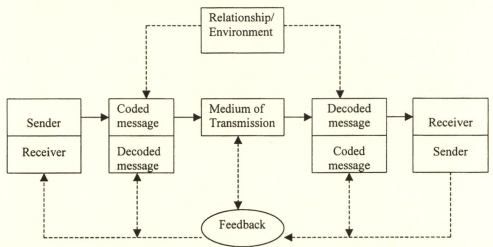

This process of transforming thoughts into a sequence of symbols is called encoding. When encoding, the source should consider the characteristics of the receiver. The symbols used should be familiar to the receiver and viewed positively. Just as important, the message must be delivered through a medium that the receiver uses and at an opportune time. Delivering the same message through two different media can produce very different results. Possible media may be classified as either personal or nonpersonal.

Although the receiver does not initiate the communication process, the receiver is just as much a communicator as the sender. The receiver communicates with the sender through feedback. The same set of symbols available to the sender is available for feedback. When the receiver provides feedback to the sender, they have reversed roles: The receiver is now the sender. Sometimes feedback is explicit and entails word, pictures, or overt signs or gestures. On other occasions, feedback is implicit and could entail subtle glances or even no response. The latter is certainly the case with mass communication, especially advertising, where feedback is implicit and delayed. When feedback is implicit and delayed, it is difficult to gauge whether the sender has effectively communicated. The nature of the feedback is determined by how well the receiver decodes, or interprets, the message delivered by the sender.

Several factors affect decoding. The nature of the relationship between the sender and receiver is one such factor. A note to a family member, for example, would be far less formal than a letter to a potential customer. Likewise, the environment in which the communication takes place can influence communication. The environment can be internal or external. The internal environment includes the inherent characteristics of the communicators, such as their experiences, attitudes, values, and biases. The external environment consists of factors outside the communicators—the weather, time of day, competing messages, and so on. Whenever the relationship between the communicators or environmental factors distort the communication process, the distortion is called interference (noise).

Types of Communication Systems

Several types of communication systems exist. They vary in complexity, level of contact between communicators, time lag of feedback, and the ability of communicators to adjust to feedback (see Table 9.1).

Interpersonal Communication Systems

The basic level of communication systems is called interpersonal communication. An interpersonal communication system may consist of as few as two people or two major subsystems; the upper level of complexity for interpersonal communication is limited only by the ability of all participants to interact with each other face to face and to have the opportunity to affect each other.

When the system consists of just two people or major subsystems, it is called a dyad. As the system becomes more complex and more subsystems are added, the small group emerges. The upper limit of the small group is usually between fifteen and twenty people. If more people are involved, the group must impose artificial regulations on itself, such as parliamentary procedure. Interpersonal communication is also affected by mediating delivery. That is, a salesperson talking face to face to a customer is engaging in direct communication. That same salesperson delivering the same message via telephone, letter, or fax is mediating the communication process by using technology. To a certain extent, using such technology limits the advantages of interpersonal communication.

Personal selling occurs within the interpersonal framework. This close contact between communicators allows some important advantages. The salesperson is able to customize the sales message to suit the audience, receives immediate feedback, and can adjust the message accordingly. The message itself can be complex, since

Table 9.1
Types of Communication Systems and Their Characteristics

Types	Characteristics			
	Complexity	Contact	Time lag	Adjustment
Interpersonal	Low	High	Short	High
Organizational	Moderate	Moderate	Moderate	Moderate
Public	High	Low	Long	Moderate
Mass	High	Low	Long	Low

explanation is possible. Unfortunately, communicating interpersonally also brings disadvantages. It is very time consuming, and some members of the target audience will be missed. That is, some interested consumers are not going to be reached by the salesperson because they are inaccessible or because there simply is not enough time to call on all customers. Salespeople working for Eli Lilly and Company, for example, attempt to call on 50 percent of their customers once each month, 25 percent once each six months, and contact 25 percent by letter or telephone two or three times annually.

Organizational Communication Systems

In a bank, factory, retail store, or government, communication is much more complex than in an interpersonal system. Each has an organizational communication system, which is composed of a large collection of subsystems all organized around common goals. The subsystems all exist as separate entities yet interrelate with each other. Consequently, both a formal and an informal network of communication is often required.

To communicate effectively in an organizational system, managers must learn as much as possible about the organizations with which they communicate. Furthermore, their messages should include common benefits desired by the majority of these organizations.

Public Communication Systems

A public communication system usually involves communication from one person to a large group of people, as occurs when a person gives a speech to an audience. Although everyone affects everyone else to some degree in every communication system, in public communication the speaker does most of the talking and has the primary effect on the people who are listening. The feedback available to the speaker is less obvious and more subtle than the feedback provided in interpersonal and organizational systems. The speaker needs considerable sensitivity to detect this feedback which is frequently nonverbal and includes facial expressions or bodily postures assumed by listeners. Some of the greatest disasters following a crisis occurred because the company spokesperson did not have the capacity to show empathy or compassion.

Mass Communication Systems

Compared with public communication, mass communication offers even less opportunity for people to interact freely with one another or to affect one another mutually. Although there is feedback in mass communication (through such means as letters, phone calls, and coupons), the distinguishing characteristic of this system is that all feedback is delayed. In such a system, the originator of the mass message cannot possibly receive feedback from all the people who receive the message. Managers must therefore establish a formal feedback system that constantly monitors the feeling, attitudes, and behaviors of audience members. They should never assume that because they hear nothing from the audience that everything is fine. The necessity for a formal feedback system may change with the emergence of technology such as the two-way video.

Persuasive Communication

People communicate in an endless number of ways, almost constantly. In business, however, one specific type of communication is primary: persuasion. Even if an individual communication piece is intended to reach an intermediate objective, such as to deliver information, remind, or build awareness, the explicit goal of the entire strategy is to persuade. In the case of public relations, persuasion may take a longer time and require several intermediate steps. When one person's achievement of a goal is blocked by the goal-seeking behavior of others, persuasion can be used to convince those others to redefine their goals or alter their means of achieving them. Thus persuasion attempts to reduce the estrangement between parties while still changing behavior; it aims for mutually satisfying results.

To ensure that all of the components of the business work toward overall objectives, each component is guided by a set of communication objectives. Some of these objectives may be very subtle, but together, they should all work to create a change in behavior.

Effective persuasion requires sensitivity to the logic of others. The persuader must locate some common ground with the audience. Thus the persuader must understand the thought processes of others. How do people process information? How do they make decisions? How does persuasion take place? We discussed theories that attempt to answer these questions in previous chapters. In the next part of this chapter, we look at the variables that can alter the outcome of a particular persuasive effort. These variables can be placed in one of three categories: source factors, message factors, and audience factors.

Characteristics of the Source

The source of a message is the speaker, communicator, or endorser— the person whose message is directed at the audience. To be more precise, we can distinguish three types of sources. The sponsor source is the manufacturer who pays for the message and is usually identified somewhere in the message itself. The reseller source is either a wholesaler or retailer that associates its name with the message. The message presenter is the person who delivers the actual message. Thus, one newspaper ad promoting AT&T telephone equipment contains the AT&T name (the sponsor source), the name of a local discount store carrying the product (the reseller source), and a picture of Cliff Robertson (the message presenter). But research on persuasive communications does not distinguish among these types of sources, so we will simply refer to all three as the source.

What makes one source more effective in persuasive communications than another? In 1983, Chrysler introduced a series of ads using a source that had rarely been used in the past. The ads featured the CEO of the company, Lee Iacocca. Iacocca proved to be an extremely effective source. Chrysler Corporation, plagued by poor products and ineffective management, was on the verge of bankruptcy, and few industry experts felt it would last the year. Thanks to Iacocca's personal plea, the situation improved; the American public began to empathize with Chrysler. Why? Iacocca apparently had high levels of three characteristics that contribute to persuasiveness: credibility, attractiveness, and power.

Credibility

The extent to which the receiver perceives the source to be truthful or believable is called source credibility. Highly credible sources tend to create an immediate change in attitude. Highly credible groups (such as the American Medical Association) are even more effective sources than highly credible individuals.

Credibility depends on two related factors. The first is the expertise attributed to the source. Characteristics such as intelligence, knowledge, maturity, and professional or social status all lend an air of expertise to an individual or group. The second factor determining credibility is the objectivity attributed to the source—in other words, the receiver's assessment of how willing the source is to discuss the subject honestly. For example, Michael Jordan and Bo Jackson are highly credible sources for athletic shoes, while former Surgeon General C. Everett Koop was a highly credible source in a public service announcement advising people to stop smoking. Objectivity seems to be less important than knowledge or expertise, however, perhaps because most people do not expect the sponsor of a message to be objective. Obviously, Michael Jordan is being paid to promote Air Jordans.

Despite the importance of expertise in determining credibility, the source should not be too perfect and should exhibit human flaws. Why? Perhaps the perfect source is too obviously a fabrication, or perhaps perfection detracts from a second determinant of persuasiveness: source attractiveness.

Attractiveness

The greater the perceived attractiveness of the source, the more persuasive the message. Source attractiveness is the extent to which the receiver identifies with the source. It results from similarity, familiarity, or likability.

Research suggests that the more receivers feel that a source is similar to themselves, or how they would like to think of themselves, the more likely they are to be persuaded. This similarity can be exhibited through ideologies, attitudes, and behaviors. Political candidates are experts at saying the right things to various audiences in order to make themselves appear similar to each audience.

The second source of attractiveness, familiarity, is normally created through past association. People have been seeing Bill Cosby for many years. He appears in concerts, on records, on television, and at charity fundraisers. Children especially relate to him, because he is funny and one of the most patient, loving, and unusual fathers ever to appear on television.

Power

In addition to credibility and attractiveness, power can make a source attractive. Power depends on the receiver's perception that the source has the ability to administer rewards or punishments. It has three components: perceived control, perceived concern, and perceived scrutiny. For example, salespeople gain perceived control over prospective customers through their knowledge of the product or access to important benefits not available to the customer directly. Many public relations efforts try to create the idea that the sponsoring company feels concern for members of the audience. IBM asks us to have a positive attitude toward the company because it is concerned with preserving the arts in America. Government agencies, banks, employment agencies, and other organizations attain power through their perceived ability to scrutinize our lives. A letter from the Internal Revenue Service is quickly opened and carefully read.

Word of Mouth: An Indirect Source

Most individuals seek information from a variety of sources outside the sponsoring organization. These external sources may be formally set up to distribute information (for example, the Small Business Administration), may provide information in line with their expertise (for example, doctors, investment analysts, and auto mechanics), or they may be individuals whose opinion is trusted on a particular topic (such as family, friends, neighbors, or coworkers). The last two sources provide what is commonly called word-of-mouth information. Unlike the producer, reseller, or spokesperson, word-of-mouth sources do not benefit from the acceptance of the message and are not under the control of the sponsor.

The impact of negative word of mouth has also been well documented. The scandal associated with Shearson Lehman Brothers and the conviction of top strategist Ivan Boesky for insider trading had a devastating effect on that organization. Negative word of mouth in the form of rumors was particularly harmful to a firm like Shearson, where trust is mandatory. Within days of Boesky's conviction, most of Shearson's regional offices were closed and hundreds of employees were fired.

Not all problems generate negative word of mouth. When is it likely? Albert Hirschman proposed a model that suggests some answers. According to Hirschman, a dissatisfied customer may make one of three responses: (1) exit—voluntary termination of the relationship, (2) voice—any attempt to change rather than escape from an objectionable state of affairs by directing dissatisfaction at management or anyone willing to listen, and (3) loyal—the customer continues with the dissatisfying product or seller and suffer in silence confident that things will soon get better.

The response a customer selects depends on the characteristics of both the individual and the industry. The key individual characteristics are (1) the perceived probability that complaining would help, (2) the worthwhile (costs benefits) of complaining, and (3) the sophistication of the consumer such as his or her awareness of a mechanism for making a complaint. The industry characteristics are essentially structural. Is the industry concentrated, highly competitive, or a loose monopoly? Negative word of mouth is most likely in concentrated industries and least likely in loose monopolies. For example, there is a great deal of negative word of mouth in the automobile industry but very little in the nursery plant industry, when three or four growers control the entire output of house plants sold in the United States. Hirschman's model has been empirically tested and appears to accurately portray the likelihood of negative word of mouth.

Message Variables

The specific elements used to communicate an idea and the way these elements are organized constitute the message variables. Message variables are divided into two categories: structure and content.

Message Structure

The overall context and readability of the message provides its structure. Aspects of message structure include whether it is verbal or nonverbal, readability, and the order of the ideas, repetition, and the presence or absence of counterarguments.

Verbal versus nonverbal. When we think about delivering a message, we think about using words, or being verbal. Speech can be powerful. It can make us laugh, cry, or feel terrified. Is a picture worth a thousand words? According to a study conducted by Ogilvy and Mather, in a given message the words create 15 percent of the impact, the tone creates 25 percent of the impact, and the graphics create 60 percent of the impact. In his excellent book, *Nonverbal Communication*, Stephen Weitz develops five categories of nonverbal communications: (1) facial expression and visual interaction (for example, eye contact), (2) body movement and gestures (such as muscle tightening and movement toward or away), (3) paralanguage (for example, loudness, pitch, and tremor of the voice), (4) proximity behaviors (for example, appropriate distance between people for certain activities), and (5) multichannel communication (such as simultaneous interaction between various factors operating in particular communication).

For persuasive appeals, the most effective nonverbal cues are facial and vocal behavior and timing of phrases, elements that the message designer clearly controls. More specifically, one study of several nonverbals used in a television commercial found that those communicating simplicity or single-mindedness were positively associated with persuasion. For example, nonverbals that correlated strongly with persuasibility included the characters' hands at their sides, the principal character expressing contentment, a likable spokesperson, a humorous mood, a busy setting, and a wink.

Readability. If we concentrate on the verbal elements of a message, it is critical that the message is readable. Readable messages are understandable to the audience and have a very good chance of being persuasive. What makes a message readable? Important factors include the arrangement words in the core message, word frequency, and sentence length. In addition, the number of ideas used to construct the core message should be kept to a minimum, and these ideas should be restated throughout the message.

Ordering effect. Should the primary ideas be presented at the beginning, middle, or end of the message? Research indicates the following:

1. When contradictory information is provided in a single message by a single source, disclaimers at the end of a message will generally be ineffective.
2. If people already feel a strong need for a product or service, supportive information should be provided first.
3. Points that are most valued by the receiver should be listed first.
4. Unfavorable information should be placed last.

In summary, the earlier the key message points are presented, the better they will be remembered.

Repetition. Repetition can take place within a message (repeating a key word or phrase), or it can be the entire message. Research suggests that repeating a message increases its believability, regardless of its content. The optimum number of repetitions is still being debated. There is general agreement that one exposure is ineffective and that three may represent the maximum number, with effectiveness quickly falling off beyond three. This generalization, however, may only be true with a captive audience, because mere exposure to a message does not guarantee attention or comprehension.

In fact, repetition can even be harmful. The results of one study suggested that repetition actually reduced comprehension. Excessive repetition may create wearout. This is evident in the case of humorous messages.

Repeating a point within a single message also seems to have a positive effect on persuasion. Several studies have shown that repeating the same point in a message facilitates retention and increases believability, regardless of the presence or absence of evidence to the contrary. Again, the ideal number of repetitions is uncertain, and it is possible to create wearout within the message itself.

Arguing and counterarguing. A one-sided message presents an argument for the sponsor without mentioning counterarguments. Using this approach is beneficial when the audience is generally friendly, when the advertiser position is the only one that will be presented, or when the desired rest is immediate through temporary opinion change. One-sided arguments tend to reinforce the decisions of the audience and do not confuse them with alternatives.

In contrast, a two-sided message includes counterarguments. In general, a two-sided argument is useful with better-educated audiences, who view counterarguments as being more objective and therefore more honest. Educated audiences are aware of opposing points of view and expect communicators to acknowledge and refute these views. Also, if audience members are likely to hold multiple opinions that touch on topics important to them, counterarguments improve persuasibility.

Message Content

The specific words, pictures, and other devices employed in a message along with the overall appeal reflect the content of the message. A very general way of analyzing message content divides messages into just two categories: rational appeals and emotional appeals. A rational appeal tends to be factual and follows a prescribed logic. In contrast, an emotional appeal is directed toward the individual's feelings and is intended to create a certain mood such as guilt, joy, anxiety, or self-pride. This distinction between rational and emotional is somewhat misleading, however, because emotions and thoughts are not things we can place in locked boxes. When someone appeals to our emotions, our cognitive processes still affect our reactions. And even nonemotional appeals may arouse strong feelings in some people. An example of an emotional appeal is demonstrated in the case depicting the Texas A&M bonfire disaster.

Audience Factors

Are some people easier to persuade than others? We all know gullible individuals who will believe anything. Yet there is little solid evidence to support the notion that there is a general personality trait for persuasibility.

Various personal characteristics, however, can affect persuasibility by affecting the recipient's comprehension of a message and willingness to comply with the message. Self-esteem is one example. For reasons yet to be explained, people with low and high self-esteem differ in their ability to cope with simple and complex information. That is, people with low self-esteem may do better with simple information and people with high self-esteem may handle complex information better.

Gender is the lone demographic trait related to persuasion. While the findings are somewhat mixed, most researchers find that women seem more persuadable than men, especially when the source is female. There is also growing evidence that males and females differ in their information-processing strategies. Moreover, it appears that there are gender differences in their thresholds for elaborative processing. In comparison with males, females seem to be more likely to elaborate message cues that command a somewhat limited amount of attention.

There have been concerns that children and senior citizens are generally more persuadable. It has been assumed that children, in particular, are very vulnerable to the effects of persuasive communication. Children's vulnerability to persuasive communication is a vast area of research in which many important questions have been considered. Do children pay attention to advertising? Do they understand its purpose and its content? How do children process messages? What is the impact of factors such as age, race, or parental education on these process effects?

CASE 9: A CRUSHING BLOW

No college tradition is stronger than the Texas A&M bonfire, preceding the annual football game with archrival University of Texas. Yet, this tradition has temporarily come to an end as a result of the disaster at 2:30 A.M. on November 23, 1999. While seventy-five students were working on the bonfire structure, there was a creaking noise, and in a matter of seconds tons of wood came rushing down like a cresting wave. Realizing friends were trapped inside, students screamed: "Get in there! Get in there!" There was little they could do. In an instant, the pride of the Aggies had crashed to earth, killing at least twelve students and injuring dozens more.

To most people outside College Station, Texas, the giant bonfire sounded like a reckless tradition—and a wasteful way to die. But to the fiercely loyal students and the school's alumni, building the bonfire was an act of faith. But the catastrophe at A&M seemed to raise old questions about college traditions and big-time athletic programs and whether the passion that fuels them is out of control.

Suddenly, a great deal of new information emerged. In 1989, a student–faculty study raised safety concerns about the bonfire and recommended cutting back on the drinking among the students building it and shortening the bonfire's height. In the late 1980s, some fifty to eighty-five students were reportedly treated each year for bonfire-related injuries. One bonfire actually collapsed in 1994, when wet ground shifted, but no one was hurt.

For the first time since President Kennedy's assassination, the bonfire was canceled. School officials chose their words carefully; a flurry of lawsuits seemed all but inevitable. And yet, on campus there appeared to be widespread agreement that the ritual was not the culprit. "It's a tragedy this fall and lives were lost," said John Slack, a senior cadet. "But it would be a tragedy to the students if it weren't allowed to continue."

Observation

When an event has created such emotional responses, as did the bonfire accident, it is difficult to communicate in a rational manner.

CONCLUSION

Crises management is inherently communication. As both a proactive and reactive process, good communication leads the way. Communicating the right message, to the right audience, at the right time is even more difficult under crisis mode. Therefore, being an excellent communicator is mandatory.

10

Communicating in a Crisis

The trick in eating crow is to pretend it tastes good.
                                                    William Safire

TYLENOL TELLS ALL

In 1982, seven people in Chicago died from cyanide-tainted Tylenol. The product tampering did not occur in the company's facilities, yet the product faced almost certain commercial demise due to the scare. The company was able to make an unprecedented comeback through the implementation of a savvy crisis communication plan. They immediately took responsibility for protecting consumers by getting the product off the shelves and halting production and advertising for the product. They also went public, warning consumers not to use the product until the source of the product tampering could be determined.

Throughout the ordeal, Johnson & Johnson executives communicated the message that the company is candid, contrite and compassionate, committed to solving the murders and protecting the public. This message rang true to consumers when the company not only sacrificed more than $100 million worth of its Tylenol product, but also put up a reward for the capture of the killer. These efforts and some strategic marketing maneuvers helped the Tylenol brand bounce back in record time, and entrenched the positive reputation of Johnson & Johnson for years to come.

The crisis communication strategy employed by Johnson & Johnson in respect to the Tylenol poisonings has been identified by experts "as the way it should be done." Once again, however, we are employing an example of a large corporation facing a catastrophe, rather than a small company dealing with a moderate inconvenience.

The new paradigm introduced in Chapter 3 indicates a much broader communication response pattern. Essentially, those contained in each cell of the matrix may require a unique communication strategy. Creating twenty-four communication strategies would prove very costly, however. Therefore, we propose a systematic crisis communication planning process be employed. This process is illustrated in Figure 10.1. The first four components are discussed in this chapter, while tactics and evaluation have their own chapter.

CRISIS COMMUNICATION PHILOSOPHY

An important starting point in your crisis communication plan is to get agreement among top management of your company regarding the overall objectives that you are trying to meet. If you have top executives who believe silence is the best method to protect the company's reputation and avoid potential lawsuits, you will need to spend a significant amount of time working to convince them that this approach can do more damage than good.

When a crisis occurs, regardless of severity, it is critical to provide factual information to your target audiences as quickly and regularly as possible to reassure them that you are taking care of the problem. If you don't communicate early and often, the rumor mill will rocket out of control and cause even more damage to the company's reputation and your customer relationships.

In addition to determining the nature of the communication response, there is also a need to decide whether your company will develop a proactive or a reactive strategy. Naturally, we advocate both; but that's still a decision to be made by top management.

Top management must also establish the tone of the crisis communication philosophy. Essentially, this refers to the attitude toward the crisis event. In the case of major catastrophes, top management at Johnson & Johnson totally accepted their responsibilities in the poisonings, and behaved accordingly. Several years later, Pepsi Cola faced a similar problem when hypodermic needles where discov-

Figure 10.1
Crisis Communication Planning

ered in several soda cans. In this case, the CEO insisted that the safety inspection procedures used at Pepsi were more than adequate and that the contamination took place somewhere else in the distribution channel. Video surveillance cameras at the store level showed that the insertion of needles was being done by consumers. Still, the tone of confidence, while risky, proved to be the most effective response.

Similar positive or negative examples can exist for much smaller businesses as well. For example, a store manager that allows sales clerks to ignore customers or treat them badly is displaying a negative tone that may be creating minor crises daily. In contrast, a restaurant manager who responds personally to every customer complaint and suggestion is displaying a positive tone intended to restrict minor crisis and prevent major ones.

Ultimately, the top management of a business or organization, regardless of size, must establish a personal philosophy about potential or actual negative events. Furthermore, this philosophy must permeate the entire organization. The old adage, "don't sweat the small stuff," could prove to be a formula for disaster.

CRISIS COMMUNICATION OBJECTIVES

As indicated in Chapter 4, establishing specific objectives is a beneficial planning activity. In the case of the crises communication process, the following sequential objectives are most common: recall and awareness, relevance and understanding, attitude change, and action.

Recall and Awareness

Learning theory tells us that the first thing that must happen for learning to take place is to get the attention of the receiver or listener. In advertising, this is accomplished through the use of several devices, including a celebrity, music, or intriguing photography, to name but a few. However, advertising is fortunate in that it can contain lots of creative and entertaining elements, far different from the normal communication. Most communication is not nearly as interesting and gaining attention is often difficult. How do we get the target audience to pay attention to safety instructions delivered by a stewardess; or listen to a lecture on investing; or heed the information of the human resources director on the possibility of downsizing? The use of fear appeals, humor, or the CEO as spokesperson are likely to gain more attention, but even these tactics are no guarantee.

Surrogate measures of attention are *recall* and *awareness*. Both have been used in advertising for many years and the resulting measures can be applied to any form of communication, including crisis communication.

Recall would ask audience members if they remember seeing or hearing the message. *Awareness* might ask about recall and also ask about details. Thus, we might desire a recall score of 50 percent, and a 30 percent awareness of the sponsor's name and primary message.

Relevance and Understanding

Once your attention has been gained, it's important to tell you something important that has relevance and understanding to you. This is accomplished through research. You might start with a list of members of your target audience and then assess what they care about, relative to your company. For example, what do your employees care about? Losing their job? Personal security? Salary? Retirement? How about your current customers? Past customers? Potential customers? Providing good value sounds like a clear concept, but it is quite complex. What words and visuals do you use in your messaging that means good value to members of your target audience? Do you provide technical information? Cost comparisons? Testimonials? Again, related fields such as sociology, psychology, and marketing have developed measures that identify both needs and level of understanding.

Level of understanding speaks to several of the communication elements discussed in the previous chapter. Using the right words, employing a rational versus emotional appeal, or focusing on visuals versus verbals are all tactics capable of enhancing the audience members level of understanding.

Measuring relevance and level of understanding is a bit more difficult than measuring attention. For one thing, relevance is often a moving target, even though the primary need may be fairly stable. For instance, an employee may need job security, and would like constant feedback via weekly memos on employee status. After a few weeks, however, the employee assumes he or she is not getting reliable information through these memos and seeks alternative sources of information. Management must monitor these need changes. Similarly, the reason the employee now mistrusts the content of these memos is because of the vague terminology found in this venue. Terms that are not familiar to the employee may confuse. There are techniques that measure understanding, but implementing such measures may prove quite expensive given the expected payoff.

Attitude Change

In an earlier chapter, we discussed attitudes; what they are, how they are formed, and how they are changed. Essentially, an attitude is a strong positive or negative feeling or belief toward a person, object, or idea. Attitudes are often created as a result of a crisis event. Bad things, as perceived by an individual, produce an emotional response, usually negative. Fire someone and they're likely to hold a negative attitude toward the company or the person who fired them, regardless of the level of justification for the firing. Treat someone poorly on your 800-hotline, and a negative attitude is likely. Conversely, counsel that same person in a caring and intelligent manner and a positive attitude is likely.

So, the "Do you want to be a millionaire" question is put simply: How do you change a negative attitude into a positive attitude? There are certain truths that affect the answer to this question. First, people do not hold strong positive or negative attitudes toward most things, people, or ideas. In fact, for the most part we are rather neutral toward most things, people, and ideas. Therefore, be careful not to assume that everyone out there is holding a negative attitude toward some behavior you demonstrate. A case in point was the neutral response of the average U.S. citizen to former President Clinton's personal behavior. Again, conducting primary research may be the only way to assess the actual level of an attitude held by a group or specific person.

A second truth is that it is very difficult to change strong positive or negative attitudes. A case in point is politics and the emotional issues related to a particular political party. Pro-life versus pro-choice has been around for over two decades with very little attitudinal resolve. Therefore, it may be a waste of time to try to change a strong positive or negative attitude. Be prepared for the long haul and the possibility that a great deal of company resources will be expended.

A final truth is that attitudes can be preempted through a targeted communication strategy. This refers to a company's or organization's ability to establish goodwill with a particular target audience so that when negative events occur, members of the target audience will tend to be more forgiving and understanding. There is even a strategy called inoculation theory that posits that if you give someone a little bit of the disease (warning about the event) it will prevent contracting the full-scale disease (crisis). In crisis communication, this theory would suggest that you inform the target audience about possible negative events, so that if they do occur the target audience is not as surprised. The whole notion of a proactive crisis communication strategy follows this idea of establishing goodwill. In this case, the focus is on controlling attitudes rather than preventing physical harm, for instance.

Action

Creating action is the most difficult objective for crisis communication to accomplish. Evidence suggests that only a small percentage of customers actually respond to product recalls. How many people actually read the safety instructions that come with products? Millions of people are injured every year because they use a product improperly and because of their general inertia toward preventive action.

Changing behavior works best when the people who are being asked to change are encouraged to participate in formulating the behavioral goals. Top-down information campaigns in most companies are doomed to failure. On the other hand, if members of the public become partners in the planning, they share ego involvement in the push for a successful outcome; and self-persuasion is a major ingredient.

A good example of action creation is the campaign by the Crime Prevention Coalition, using McGruff the Crime Dog and the slogan "Taking a Bite Out of Crime." The program had been implemented through local police departments, which handle the campaign materials—videos, brochures, and other information—on how to protect yourself from crime. These efforts, reinforced by a media campaign, show McGruff dressed in a fedora and trench coat. The dog is a favorite with children, who take messages home from school and also take part in the water program. Quite a bit of action has been prompted through this message strategy.

CRISIS COMMUNICATION TARGET AUDIENCES

In an earlier chapter we introduced the term "stakeholder" to represent individuals or organizations that have specific expectations from the business and that the business owes them some level of accountability. We now address a subset of the stakeholder group—the target audience. The target audience reflects those individuals or organizations that you wish to communicate with. It may include all stakeholders, or some part. This group may be further reduced when we identify those that the crisis manager wants to communicate with. For example, the manager of a local landscaping firm may wish to communicate with all forty-five employees about fringe benefits, schedules, and training; but training may be particularly relevant to the twenty-nine employees who actually use the most dangerous equipment.

It is also possible that the target audience is larger than the group of stakeholders. This is fairly common when a crisis event occurs and the company wishes to communicate with the general public, a government agency, or the media.

Knowing as much about your target audience is a necessary prerequisite for effective crisis communication. Again, the need to conduct secondary and primary research is imminent, as is the need to make sure the research findings are particularly useful in your efforts to communicate effectively. Factors discussed in the previous chapter, such as clarity, relevance, and the right media are all important.

CRISIS COMMUNICATION STRATEGIES

How are we going to persuade customers to read instructions? Despite the efforts of major pharmacies to include elaborate warnings about dosage, harmful combinations, and timing, their efforts often go unheeded. Ditto to efforts by computer manufacturers who outline a plethora of instructions for the care of their laptops. Of course these examples represent proactive tactics. Imagine how much more difficult it is to communicate under duress.

Developing effective crisis communication strategies is a direct result of the stated objectives, along with the target audiences specified. In the case of crisis communications there are two additional factors to consider: proactive and reactive, and crisis-specific factors.

Proactive and Reactive Factors

We have already discussed the differences between proactive versus reactive strategies. These two perspectives have a direct bearing on the company's communication efforts. Most notably, proactive communication tends to identify areas of potential crisis and tries to eliminate or diminish the likelihood of it occurring. Forewarning consumers of potential dangers when using a product is an example of this strategy. In addition, proactive communication may focus on creating goodwill or trust. Creating goodwill and/ or trust is not easy and may take a great deal of time and energy to establish in the mind of the target audience. Above all, it requires consistency on the part of the business, during good times and bad. A garage that is willing to tow your car in for free can create a great deal of goodwill. Likewise, a home remodeling company that guarantees their work for one year and shows up on time creates an unusual level of trust. As noted earlier, creating goodwill and trust greatly increases the likelihood that the target audience will be more understanding and forgiving when negative events do occur. More will be said about proactive strategies later in this chapter.

Reactive crisis communication strategies have clearly been the focus for those responsible for crisis management. Many of the recommendations emerging from this area are applicable to proactive strategies as well. A review of the major ideas follows.

1. *Create an open communication system.* In planning for a crisis, always recognize that information is going to be in great demand. You can make a crisis easier to handle, though, if you organize the information you can obtain in advance. You should collect information on products and services, processes, locales, people, and the policies that govern the organization. Keep all this information readily available to those most likely to need it, and keep it in a form that is most likely to be usable in a crisis.

2. *Create a basic crisis-communication information book.* Such a book should contain the following:
   - addresses, telephone numbers, other contact information for all major offices, branches, and subsidiaries
   - descriptions of all facilities, along with a list of all people working in each area, escape routes, safe areas, and so on

- biographical information on all employees, especially key executives
- photos of all facilities and all principals
- statistics on the facilities and the institutions, including a history of the institution
- a list of emergency contact numbers and people
- a format for accounting for each member of the workforce

3. *Communicate the crisis plan to all employees, via easy-to-use facts sheets and background information.*

4. *Assemble and maintain a crisis team.* This team will generate message statements (often instructed by an outside public relations firm); should be isolated from some day-to-day activities; designate members of the team as fact-finders; designate members of the team as evaluators, include legal counsel; designate and train spokespersons.

5. *Use employees effectively in a crisis.* Employees are the organization's most credible representatives to the people outside the organization with whom they come in contact. People will develop perceptions from the way employees respond to their questions and from their behavior.

6. *In planning for crisis, you need to be able to anticipate the communication climate by predicting how management is likely to act and react.* Usually, these projections should be made (a) prior to the crisis during normal day-to-day operations, (b) at the moment some event triggers the crisis, and (c) during the crisis situation that follows the event.

7. *Keep an accurate record of all communication that takes place before, during, and after the crisis event.* Consequently, there must be a mechanism put in place for collecting this information. This mechanism might include news conferences, bulletins, satellite teleconferencing, Web pages, e-mail, teletext or videotext, telephone banks with 800 or 900 lines, trained responders, and so forth.

8. *Establish a positive relationship with all relevant media.* There are a host of rules and suggestions concerning how to best establish a positive relationship with the media. For example, experience suggests that the media wishes you to be honest, accessible, and as forthright as possible. Also, they need lead-time and always appreciate it when they are educated as well as informed.

In addition to these guidelines, there are two other communication-related phenomena that have been discussed in crisis communication strategy: public opinion and rumors. Both provide insights.

Public Opinion

Understanding public opinion begins with a definition of the lead term "public." The term "public" has traditionally meant any group (or possibly, individual) that has some involvement with an organization. Publics and organizations have consequences for each other: What a public does has some impact on the organization and vice versa. The following list shows that there are a great many publics, relevant and irrelevant, high priority and low priority. Publics for any organization fall into these categories, reprinted with permission from Jerry A. Hendrix, *Public Relations Cases* (Copyright 1992 Wadsworth, Inc,):

Media Publics
Mass media
    Local
        Print publications
            Newspapers
            Magazines
        TV stations
        Radio stations
    National
        Print publications
        Broadcast networks
        Wire services
Specialized media
    Local
        Trade, industry, and association publications
        Organizational house and membership publications
        Ethnic publications
        Specialized broadcast programs and stations
    National
        General business publication
        National trade, industry, and association publications
        National organizational house and membership publications
        National ethnic publications
        Publications of national special groups
        National specialized broadcast programs and networks

Employee Publics
Management
    Upper-level administrators
    Midlevel administrators
    Lower-level administrators
Nonmanagement (staff)
    Specialists

Clerical personnel
Secretarial personnel
Uniformed personnel
  Equipment operators
  Drivers
  Security personnel
  Other uniformed personnel
Union representatives
Other nonmangement personnel

Member Publics

Organization employees
  Headquarters management
  Headquarters nonmanagement staff
  Other headquarters personnel
Organization officers
  Elected officers
  Appointed officers
  Legislative groups
  Board, committees
Organization members
  Regular members
  Members in special categories—sustaining, emeritus, student
    members
  Honorary members or groups
Prospective organization members
State or local chapters
  Organization employees
  Organization officers
  Organization members
  Prospective organization members
Related or other allied organizations

Community Publics

Community media
  Mass
  Specialized
Community leaders
  Public officials

    Educators
    Religious leaders
    Professionals
    Executives
    Bankers
    Union leaders
    Ethnic leaders
    Neighborhood leaders
Community organizations
    Civic
    Service
    Social
    Business
    Cultural
    Religious
    Youth
    Political
    Special interest groups
    Other

Government Publics

Federal
    Legislative branch
      Representatives, staff, committee personnel
      Senators, staff, committee personnel
    Executive branch
      President
      White House staff, advisers, committees
      Cabinet officers, departments, agencies
      Commissions
State
    Legislative branch
      Representatives, delegates, staff, committees
      Personnel
      Senators, staff, committee personnel
    Executive branch
      Governor
      Governor's staff, advisers, committees
      Cabinet officers, departments, agencies

Commissions
County
    County executive
    Other county officials, commissions, departments
City
    Mayor or city manager
    City council
    Other city officials, commissions, departments

Investor Publics

Shareowners and potential shareowners

Security analysts and investment counselors

Financial press

    Major wire services: Dow Jones & Co., Reuters Economic Service, AP, UPI

    Major business magazines: *Business Week, Fortune,* and the like—mass circulation and specialized

    Major newspapers: *New York Times, Wall Street Journal*

    Statistical services: Standard and Poor's Corp., Moody's Investor Service, and the like

    Private wire services: PR News Wire, Business Wire

    Securities and Exchange Commission (SEC), for publicly owned companies

Consumer Publics

Company employees

Customers

    Professionals

    Middle class

    Working class

    Minorities

    Other

Activist consumer groups

Consumer publications

Community media, mass and specialized

Community leaders and organizations

International Publics

Host country media

    Mass

    Specialized

Host country leaders
    Public officials
    Educators
    Social leaders
    Cultural leaders
    Religious leaders
    Political leaders
    Professionals
    Executives
Host country organizations
    Business
    Service
    Social
    Cultural
    Religious
    Political
    Special interests
    Other

Special Publics
Media consumed by this public
    Mass
    Specialized
Leaders of the public
    Public officials
    Professional leaders
    Ethnic leaders
    Neighborhood leaders
Organizations composing this public
    Civil
    Political
    Service
    Business
    Cultural
    Religious
    Youth

For instance, employees, women, and minorities are often viewed as high priority publics. Employees are always an important public because they are any organization's "front line." Employees are seen as knowledgeable about the organization with the special insight of an insider's experience and information, so they are credible to other publics. Also, employees often have direct contact with other publics, such as customers or suppliers. Women and minorities may be part of an employee public, but additionally, from a broader perspective, they constitute significant publics who can damage an institution's reputation. Insensitivity to women and minorities in all types of relationships has cost profit and nonprofit groups both money and status.

Bernard Hennessey says, "Public opinion is the complex of preferences expressed by a significant number of persons on an issue of general importance." Hennessey, who does not distinguish between opinion and attitude, says that public opinion has five basic elements. First, public opinion must be focused on an issue. Second, the public must consist of a recognizable group of persons concerned with the issue. A third element of the definition, the phrase "complex of preferences" means more than mere direction and intensity; it means all the imagined or measured individual opinions held by all the relevant publics on all the proposals about the issue over which the public has come into existence. The fourth factor, the expression of opinion, may involve any form of expression—printed or spoken words, symbols, or even the gasp of a crowd. The fifth factor is the number of persons involved. The number of people in a public can be large or small, as long as the impact of their opinion has a measurable effect. The effect may be as much determined by the intensity of opinion and the organization of effort as by the size of the public.

Public opinion expresses beliefs not necessarily based on facts but on perceptions or evaluations of events, persons, institutions, or products. In the United States, many people assume that "public opinion is always right." Obviously, public opinion can be misused or manipulated—as Adolf Hitler's master propagandist Joseph Goebbels, demonstrated. And it can be based on a lack of accurate information—as in the period before World War II when many Americans applauded Mussolini's efforts at "straightening out the Italians."

Public opinion also is notably unstable. That is why the bottom line for political strategists is election day itself, when the actual votes are tallied, not public opinion poll results from earlier in the campaign. Exposure to new information or events can quickly change public opinion, rendering recent polling research obsolete.

To keep pace with constantly changing public opinion, you must accept a few basic precepts. Not everyone is going to be on your side at any one time. The best you can hope for is a majority consensus.

Winning over the opposition is a most difficult task. Most of us read and listen for reinforcement of our own ideas. We do not like to hear ideas that conflict with our own, and we make every effort to reject them. For example, we may simply tune out and fail to hear or remember what we have been exposed to.

Because public opinion changes so often and can be influenced so easily, measuring it is big business. As noted in Chapter 2, both primary and secondary sources of public opinion are available. Published surveys, for instance, are available by subscription to the Roper Center for Public Opinion Research. Issues of *The Public Perspective* are also available on-line in Nexis. It often includes polls, such as those taken by Louis Harris, George Gallup, or news organizations, which sample the nation's moods and pass on the information through public outlets. Other public opinion research is offered by a variety of groups for a fee.

Managers will often perform similar research themselves, although this is proprietary—owned by the organization paying for it, and unavailable to other firms or clients. Even when no primary research is done, however, familiarity with research methodology is essential to be able to successfully apply the many published surveys to a particular company, market, or client.

Dealing with public opinion is the real challenge. Today, many publics share knowledge or work together on various issues. Hence, organizations sometimes find, to their dismay, coalitions of unlikely partners involved in a boycott or other hostile action against them. Computerized information banks, electronic mail, facsimile, video-conferencing and special-interest organizations create loosely affiliated publics with strong emotional ties to particular issues. Because of crossover of communication among these loosely connected publics, one must make sure that a message designed to respond to one public doesn't offend another.

Even though different publics often share some common interests and values, it is increasingly dangerous to assume that people share common sets of values. Thus, an organization trying to determine a socially responsible course of action must simultaneously try to respond to specific interest groups interested in changing broader public opinion.

Rumors

Every business or organization is susceptible to rumors; those bits of information not verified by facts. The rumor mill is quite easy to start, and quite difficult to stop. Often based on lies, exaggeration, cruel intent, or idealized intent, rumors can be either bad news or good. In either case, if enough time passes or enough people jump on the bandwagon, rumors may become facts.

Because rumors feed on anxiety, emotional topics such as threats to physical or emotional well-being are always an integral part of them. And the people most distressed by something new are the ones most likely to pass it on. The following advice is useful in avoiding rumors from starting:

1. Make sure information related to your organization is authentic, official, and as complete as possible.
2. Avoid situations that are loaded with anxiety and fear and where the likelihood of erroneous information is high.
3. Make sure that people's ego needs are being met at a reasonable level (possessing the "inside dope").
4. Minimize serious organizational problems and/or volatility.
5. Deal with issues in a timely manner.

Should a rumor get started, the following strategies are offered:

1. Analyze the scope and seriousness of the nature and impact of the rumor before planning and engaging in any active connection.
2. Analyze the specific causes, motives, sources, and dissemination of the rumors.
3. Confer with persons affected by or being damaged by rumors. Dispel the rumors.
4. Call the status and informal leaders, opinion molders, and other influential people together to discuss and clarify the situation and to solicit their support and assistance.
5. Don't attack the rumor since people often feel an extreme defensive response supports the truth of the rumor.

The case study that follows illustrates the power of a rumor.

CASE 10: IT'S A LIE!

The growth at First Baptist Church during the last eighteen months was nothing short of spectacular. Since the arrival of the new minister, Dr. Raymond Smith, the number of active members has nearly doubled from 175 families to 321 families. More important, the new families were very active, volunteering to teach Sunday School classes, singing in the choir, and mentoring youth groups.

It was this last activity that was the source of all the problems. Pam Scolder had been the adult leader for the ten- to twelve-year-old girls' groups for nearly seven months. Pam was a former physical education teacher who was injured in an auto accident four years ago, leaving her unable to walk without crutches. She lived on SSI and a small pension. To save costs, she shared a small house with Sally Bates, a secretary.

The girls at First Baptist loved Pam and thoroughly enjoyed her enthusiasm and energy, despite her handicap. They all went on outings and she often had the girls over to her home to play games, watch DVDs and just hang out.

It was on a Monday afternoon that Reverend Smith received an anonymous phone call. The caller indicated that Pam was a lesbian and was making improper advances to several of the girls. The last words from the caller were, "You'd better do something about this, and quick." By Tuesday morning a group of "concerned parents" appeared at the Reverend's door demanding that Pam be removed from her volunteer job. Later that day, he met with Pam and asked her if the rumor was true. Pam indicated that she was not required to answer, and stated, "I thought we were all Christians!" She resigned later that day and removed her name from the church membership list.

Observation

Are such rumors inevitable to a point where they are beyond the control of management?

CONCLUSION

Crisis communication remains one of the most difficult tasks for the crisis manager. Following a set process is the best chance of success. The next chapter describes some of the most popular kinds of communication tactics.

11

Crisis Communication Tactics

Wisdom is knowing what to do next; virtue is doing it.
David Jordan, *American Naturalist*

THE BIG BUG HAS ARRIVED

To improve its relationship with clients, Hewlett Packard (HP) sent e-mail newsletters to all customers who registered on-line. It gave new customers incentives like better warranties to register via its Web site. Implementation of the campaign was left to Digital Impact Inc., a Silicon Valley e-marketing company.

Digital Impact segmented HP's customer e-mail list by date-of-purchase and product, and sent customized newsletters containing information about optimizing the performance of HP products and services, including reminders about maintenance. Here's the cool part: The newsletters featured a button allowing readers to forward it to friends or colleagues. "The user clicks and sees a Web page hosted by Digital Impact for HP, where they can type in the friend's e-mail and a comment, then hit the send button," explains Wiebke Singliu, business-to-business engagement manager for Digital Impact. "The technology takes the message, inserts it above the newsletter, and e-mails the whole thing to the friend."

At the bottom of each newsletter readers are asked if they'd like to receive HP newsletters themselves. If so, they can sign up, adding their name to HP's database. Though HP's marketers may not have realized it, having its customers send newsletters to friends or colleagues is textbook viral marketing, one of the newest, cheapest ways of marketing on the Web. It involves creating an e-mail so compelling—either graphically or by using an incentive—that customers want to pass it along.

For the most part, managing crisis communication has been driven by the development of tactics. Public relations experts focus on putting on the best event, creating the best press kit, placing stories in the most prestigious publications, and training top management to be credible spokespersons. While all these are admirable tasks, they are not necessarily either strategy-based or integrated. The approach in this chapter is to discuss crisis communication tactics from a strategy perspective.

We begin with a description of the most popular crisis communication tactics and conclude with a model that will integrate these tactics.

CRISIS COMMUNICATION TACTICS

Tactics are the methods, actions, and activities used to achieve objectives. They translate the directives of strategies into specific programs. When writing the crisis communications plan, the tactics recommended should relate specifically to each strategy. The plan should specify the activities that will take place, who will do them, when they will be done, and at what cost.

Tactics are the payoff of all the strategic planning that precedes them. The best strategic plans will succeed only if the tactics capture the attention of targeted individuals. The importance of tactics cannot be overemphasized. All things being equal, they make all the difference in the world.

One of the exciting things about crisis management is that lists of tactics will continue to evolve, reflecting the creativity of its practitioners, new advances in technology, and new emphasis on reaching target individuals one-on-one as well as target groups through the media.

The advent of new technology has added a number of exciting new tactical options. The first scientific survey of the use of the Internet conducted late in 1995 by Nielsen Media Research revealed that 37 million people, or 17 percent of the population of the United States and Canada, had access to the Net. On the average, those users spent nearly five-and-a-half hours a week on-line. The numbers have tripled since then.

The uses of crisis management messaging through cyberspace are burgeoning. At this writing, literally millions of Web sites exist, providing layer upon layer of information directly to self-selected audience members. Reporters, once dependent on clippings and microfilm, can now access all they need to trace a company story on the Internet from text of published articles and the company's file of press releases, past and present. They can also find out what competitors are doing by accessing their Web sites and what consumers are saying in news groups and chat rooms.

But don't count on the early demise of traditional media. Rather than replacing traditional media, on-line media are more likely to become another, albeit particularly attractive media alternative, to at least some businesses. Radio didn't disappear when TV became the rage. It is still the medium of choice of drivers. At home, most Americans are still spending several hours a day watching television. The number of cable channels continues to proliferate.

The growth of cable has opened tremendous new opportunities for those responsible for crisis communications. The success of CNN and *Headline News* has led to another twenty-four-hour news network; Fox News Channel, as well as MSNBC. Two cable channels, CNBC and CNNFN, specialize in business news.

Let's review some of the tactics now available to crisis communications managers; both proactive and reactive.

Advertising. Advertising can be used as a crisis communication tactic to support special events or contests, announce or honor award winners, support causes, create a positive image, or reassure consumers about product safety or efficiency.

Arts and entertainment sponsorships. Corporate or brand sponsorship of art exhibits and the performing arts are growing in prominence with the reduction of government support of the arts. They offer an opportunity to reach customers and influential business leaders in a noncommercial environment. Most major exhibitions and an increasing number of concert, dance, and theatrical series and events, as well as public television and radio productions, are now made possible by corporate grants.

Awards. The perception is that a brand sponsoring the award is the leader that preempts competition. Awards are frequently used in such industries as apparel or health and beauty, but are also used for broader crisis communication purposes honoring teachers, scientists, community service leaders, and heroes and heroines.

Birthdays and anniversaries. The use of significant brand birthdays to reinforce brand loyalty often can be used to announce product improvements, new sizes, new packaging, new flavors, or line extensions. This is particularly effective with long-time favorite products.

Booklets and brochures. Company-sponsored printed material that provides stakeholders with useful information is referred to as booklets or brochures. Information is usually but not always related to product use or the interests and lifestyles of target consumers.

Books. Books represent publications that bring attention to companies, including authorized company histories and autobiographies of company leaders and their vision for the future. Also brand-titled references and how-to books reinforce a company's expertise.

B-roll. This category reflects supplementary or backup material. It is now standard practice to include B-roll with edited video news releases to give TV editors material to build their own stories. It might include file footage of production line and products in use; interviews with celebrity spokespersons and directors of new commercials; outtakes and making of commercials; company spokespersons and industry analysts commenting on new products as well as special-event coverage.

By-line stories. These are articles written by company executives in general business publications and trade books serving their industry. Also, newspaper op-ed pages offer opportunities to present company or industry points of view to influence stakeholder attitudes and opinions.

Cause-related marketing. This technique represents corporate or brand support of causes based on product sales or transactions. Crisis communication support includes planning of media events, issuing sponsorship announcements, updates and results, and gaining editorial endorsement.

CD-ROM (Compact Disc–Read Only Memory). Optical discs and computer software are commonly used in place of or in addition to traditional printed crisis-related materials to communicate with both the media and various stakeholders. The combination of text, graphics, video, and sound adds dimension and excitement to the kinds of material traditionally used in press kits, booklets, and brochures.

Celebrity endorsements. This tactic includes celebrities as company spokespersons to deliver certain messages; sometimes as an expert as well. Such celebrities can deliver these messages through a variety of venues, including company-sponsored events, press releases, and videos.

CEOs. Often the top executive can become the most effective spokesperson for the company. This can include announcing new products, engaging in new markets, or dealing with crisis, such as Bill Gates responding to the attempted breakup of Microsoft.

Specialty advertising. There are hundred of items that carry the logo or message of a company. Examples include pins, pens, calendars, key chains, mugs, t-shirts, caps, and so forth. Some have become so popular that they have become a source of revenue, such as Hard Rock clothing, Disney paraphernalia, Harley Davidson, and Ben & Jerry's clothing.

Demonstrations. There are instances when demonstrating a product in person, on TV, or the Internet, is effective in creating interest, understanding, and acceptance. Trade shows are a particular location for conducting demonstrations. It can also prevent improper product use.

Direct mail. Thanks to the emerging sophistication of databases, reaching the right individual in a timely manner has become a reality. Direct mail can be used to deliver new information and/or respond to crisis-like events. In fact, by employing the matrix introduced in Chapter 3, various audience members can be segmented into unique crisis-related databases.

Exhibits. Exhibits can take many forms, including historical exhibits at company headquarters, product exhibits at malls, fairs, libraries, or exhibits that tie-in to users of the product, such as hospitals that use certain software. For nearly a year, IBM sponsored an exhibit at the Chicago Museum of Science and Industry. There are companies that specialize in designing, manufacturing, and erecting exhibits.

Fan clubs. Some products become so popular, or are so unique, that they inspire fan clubs. The Barbie Fan Club may be the largest in the world. There are also fan clubs for Corvettes, Ford Mustangs, and Harley motorcycles. Thanks to the Internet, companies can start and maintain fan clubs.

Festivals. Festivals are multiple-day events, held on a regular basis, sponsored by a company, person, or community. There are literally thousands of arts festivals sponsored by big and little cities throughout the world. Plano, Texas celebrates a week-long wine festival that attracts many thousands. The Hershey Company creates goodwill through their annual Chocolate Festival.

Grand opening. Opening a new business or a new branch of an existing business can serve as an effective proactive strategy for the crisis manager. Creating elaborate events, bringing in celebrities, inviting best customers and local dignitaries, and creating a charitable event can be quite effective. Again, arranging for a grand opening may be best left to a professional, since there are many tasks to be completed.

Green marketing. Green marketing is a term coined in the 1970s that reflected the attempt by business to be more environmentally aware and friendly. Companies that don't pollute, recycle, and create products that are biodegradable found that a large sector of society would purchase from them just for being green. Unfortunately, this trend has diminished somewhat and companies that engage in green marketing do it because it is good business.

Guideline and direction kits. There are several industries and/or companies that provide their stakeholders with direction kits that enhance the use of their products. Examples include utility companies that provide kits demonstrating how to test the tightness of their home, how to insulate properly, and how to reduce utility costs. Car manufactures, such as Subaru, provide a very detailed kit showing how to install a baby seat.

Hotlines. Both 800-numbers (free) and 900-numbers (small cost) have become a given for most companies. Calls are personally handled in most cases, but advances in technology have made it possible to provide answers to a variety of frequently asked questions via recorded messages. The Butterball Turkey Talk-Line dispenses advice on how to thaw a turkey, cook it, tell when it's done, and how to carve it. Hotlines are particularly important in managing crisis; they are best matched to the classification matrix.

Interviews. One-on-one interviews have the potential to either diminish or exacerbate a crisis event. Making sure the person who represents the company is appropriate, articulate, and properly trained is necessary. There may even be a decision to create specialists within the company; by topic, media, or length of interview. This needs to be part of the proactive crisis plan.

Junkets. There are instances when it is beneficial to take selected stakeholders, media, or even government officials on free trips to out-of-town locations. It may be the only way media can afford to cover an event or story. A rumor can be quickly squelched if relevant stakeholders are allowed to "see for themselves." A high-risk destination, such as Iraq or Nigeria, can only convince travel agents it is safe by paying for them to visit.

Mat releases. Mat releases are materials for newspaper delivered in camera-ready format. Mats are used for new-product stories, feature stories, pictorial features, byline columns, and editorials. The material is particularly suitable for weekly and community newspapers. Mat release services now distribute material on compact discs and have Web sites from which reporters can download mat material.

Media tours. There are instances when a company spokesperson tours several cities or countries in order to gain access to local media. This is quite common for book authors and movie stars. Companies have also joined the ranks of spokespersons who are booked on radio and television talk shows, or at local events.

News conferences. News conferences are an integral part of most communication strategies, especially crisis communication. News conference implies both print and broadcast media. They are used to announce significant information to the media.

News groups. The Internet has introduced a whole new category of communication systems, such as news groups, chat groups, and chat rooms. They represent people who have common interests and are used by companies to monitor what stakeholders are saying about their products and services and those of their competitors.

Newsletters. Companies and trade groups have adapted the newsletter format to keep their products top-of-mind and communicate news and views to stakeholders on a regular basis. They may include coupons and rebates, but typically update the reader on company news.

News release (press release). This remains the primary vehicle for the organization to communicate with it stakeholders. The news release is written in journalistic news style covering who, what, when, where, and why, with the most important news at the top of the story. News releases are distributed at news conferences or transmitted to the media directly or by commercial news wire services. Most companies now post their news releases on their Web sites.

Photographs and photo opportunities. Identifying opportunities for interesting photographic events is a full-time job for some companies. A good wire service photo may appear in hundreds of newspapers. Although most magazines use their own photography, there are still instances when company-provided photos are accepted.

Plant tours. Some plants provide interesting tours for a variety of stakeholders. Examples include Coors Brewing, the Hershey Company, Ben & Jerry's ice cream plant, and the Steuban tour at Corning Glassworks. Plant tours can be an excellent way to involve people and products. At the end of the tours, there is usually an opportunity to sample and/or buy products.

Press kits. Press kits are used in conjunction with events where the media are invited. It includes all the information the reporter will need to cover the story, including news releases, fact sheets, feature stories, and photographs. In some cases, the kit may include video news releases and B-rolls, sales literature, advertising proofs, or CD-ROMS.

Product placements. Placement of products in movies and on television shows is becoming very popular. Movies such as *Independence Day* and *The Flintstones*, and TV shows such as *Seinfeld* and *Will & Grace* have featured a variety of products, either as part of the plot or just for fun.

Public service announcements (PSAs). PSAs are television and radio messages that are run free of charge by stations in public service time, usually at the end of the broadcast day. Some companies underwrite the production of PSAs for nonprofits organizations. PSAs can represent national issues or can be used to promote local events supporting local charities.

Reprints. Reprints of articles that have appeared in public or trade publications can be sent to specific stakeholders or used as door openers for salesmen. Case histories that include customer endorsements or byline articles that convey the implied endorsement of the publication can be a major communication success.

Road shows. Some companies take their show on the road to major markets to introduce management and showcase current and future products to customers and other key stakeholders. These events might include a variety of stakeholders, including dealers, wholesalers, shareholders, employees, retirees, and customers. In addition to product displays and demonstrations, multimedia and interactive exhibits can be used to dramatize the company's research and development and operations.

School programs. There are many companies who supplement classroom materials. A typical package might include student activity books, a classroom poster, an educational video, a teacher's guide, and suggested lesson plans. Food companies may donate food or cut a deal to sell items to students. Banks also have introduced student programs and explain how banking works.

Seminars. Seminars represent company-sponsored events that provide opportunities for stakeholders to obtain useful information on subjects of interest from recognized experts in their fields. Examples include Home Depot, Saturn Motors, and Prudential Securities. Seminars also offer media relations opportunities such as interviews with company executives, authors, and expert panelists.

Speakers' bureaus. Any organization can form a speaker's bureau that provides speakers for civic groups, service clubs, school, clubs, and libraries. These speakers can reach a large cross-section of the population. At their appearances, they often distribute informational materials and branded mementos. These appearances offer good opportunities to collect names and addresses for database use.

Surveys. Like polls, surveys are proven ways to achieve positive media exposure. Material may be derived from market research or may be generated by the organizations. *USA Today*, for example, provides the results from several of these surveys in each issue. Nestlé Company recently conducted a national survey on women's attitudes toward breastfeeding versus formula. Surveys often denote industry leadership.

Tie-ins. When two or more noncompeting companies partner on a particular event or task they are doing a tie-in. The right commercial partner may provide borrowed interest necessary to attract media attention. Partnering with a nonprofit organization can lend credibility to the company. The American Dental Association endorsement of Crest toothpaste proved to be a very successful tie-in.

Tradeshows. Most industries have one or more tradeshows where they can introduce new products, demonstrate products, observe competitors, sell products, and meet stakeholders. Tradeshows are usually covered by relevant media, and it is not unusual for companies to plan preshow or postshow events targeted at the media. Some tradeshows, such as the major automobile shows in Detroit, Chicago, and Frankfort, are open to the public and generate widespread media coverage.

Video. Videos are one of the most versatile crisis communication tactics. In addition to video news releases, videos are used for information and educational purposes. Company-sponsored videos are frequently provided to schools and used to reach other target audiences. An athletic equipment manufacturer, Wilson Company, has produced a video that teaches schoolchildren how to prevent head injuries.

Videoconferences. Satellite transmission has facilitated the linking of sites by closed-circuit television. Videoconferencing can be used to link special events in several markets for transmission to employees, dealers, distributors, franchises, retailers, and the media. This tactic proved very effective for Microsoft when they launched Windows 95. Videoconferencing and its audio equivalent, teleconferencing is a strong consideration for crisis communication.

Web sites. Many thousands of companies and organizations have a presence on one or more Web sites. The World Wide Web can reach all kinds of stakeholders, throughout the world, instantaneously. The Web can handle text, graphics, video, and sound. Moreover, sites can be linked to many other relevant sites, creating a network advantageous to all participants.

Be cognizant of the fact that the previous discussion is just that, a discussion. If you are serious about employing any of these tactics, acquiring professional help is suggested. Bringing this expertise in-house must always be considered in light of the relative costs.

THE IMPLEMENTATION PROCESS

Identifying tactics alternatives is just a step in the crisis communication process. Combining the various tactics in a meaningful way is the real key. We offer the crisis classification matrix introduced in Chapter 3 as an initial framework for creating an implementation process. By doing this you can align a set of tactics within each cell in the matrix. This will not only create a type of synergy, it will also incorporate the dimensions of the matrix in assessing the appropriateness of a particular tactic or set of tactics relative to a particular crisis matrix cell. In addition, the dimensions found in the matrix can provide guidance in implementing the various tactics.

Figure 3.4 demonstrates how this might work. Recall that this matrix illustrated the crisis situation for a fictitious company www.lit.com. Eleven of the cells were partially completed to represent possible crisis events. If you create a framework similar to Table 11.1, you should be able to systematically select tactics, both proactive and reactive, for the various target audiences noted.

To demonstrate this process, Table 11.1 has been completed using five of the events identified in Figure 3.4 for www.lit.com. Note that under the *criteria* column, the codes listed represent the criteria found in Figure 3.4, for example, TLH, TPI, ROM, and DOCL stands for the following: threat level high, time pressure intense, response options many, and degree of control low. Thus in the case

Table 11.1
Tactical Assignment Process for Potential and Actual Crises

EVENT	CRITERIA	TARGET AUDIENCES
New Competitor	TLH, TPI, POF, DOCL	Current Customers
Rumors	TLL, TPM, ROM, DOCL	Employees, Current Customers, Media
Natural Disaster	TLL, TPM, ROF, DOCL	Employees, current/potential customers
		Media
Product Tampering	TLL, TPI, ROF, DOCL	Employees, current customers, public
		media
IPO Failure	TLH, TPM, ROF, DOCL	Employees, current customers, financial
		Community

of cell number 3, rumors, the criteria considered are the following: threat level low, time pressure moderate, response options many, and degree of control low.

Likewise, the target audiences considered as part of the crisis communication strategy were employees, current customers, and the media. All three target audiences are considered with both proactive and reactive tactics.

Let's assume that the crisis strategy employed by www.lit.com in respect to rumors is as follows.

Create a data-gathering mechanism that is able to identify, monitor, and respond to all rumors that impact www.lit.com. Several tactics are listed, both proactive and reactive.

For instance, proactive tactics include developing and distributing an in-house newsletter that deals with hot topics within the industry and the company; two kinds of suggestion boxes, the traditional wooden box and the electronic version that is part of the chat room; the creation of a comprehensive Web site that includes an intranet communication mechanism; and a 900 number that

Table 11.1 (*continued*)

COMMUNICATION TACTICS

PROACTIVE	REACTIVE
Continuity program	Product Comparison communication
Product Update Communication	Web. Special event, Fax
In-house Publication/Newsletter	Intranet, meetings, in-house
900#, intranet, Web, Sugg. box	Publication, Open house, 800#, Press kit,
Handbook, 900#, Open House	Press conf, 800#, 900#, Web, Fax
meeting	Intranet, press release, media kit
Publicity, Web, Intranet	Speech Intranet, press conf.
	800#, 900#, Web, media kit, recall
Institutional Ads, video,	Press conf., 800#, Web
Financial reports, Web,	Interviews, Direct mail,
Celebrity appearance	Media kit, Fax

allows employees, customers, and the media to get answers to their questions.

Reactive tactics are also mentioned. Several of the elements from the proactive side would also be used as reactive strategies, including the in-house newsletter and the Web or Internet system. New elements intended to be reactive include an 800 number available to the media and the public, various meetings targeted at stakeholders affected by the rumor, an open house to ease concerns related to the rumors, and a press kit distributed to the media and other relevant stakeholders. Again, all these elements would be customized to the actual rumor(s) of concern. This same process would be repeated for all the potential crisis listed in Table 11.1. It would be imperative to attempt to consider these various tactics in light of using them repeatedly. That is, in the case of our example, the Web site should be designed in light of all relevant potential crises. For the five crises listed, the Web site would play a role in each. Creating this type of synergy across tactics would save resources and increase the effectiveness of each tactic.

CONCLUSION

This chapter identified a number of tactics employed in crisis communication. Some are traditional and have been used for many years. Others are quite new and are strongly related to emerging technology. More important, this chapter views these tactics in a strategic manner, employing the classification matrix referenced throughout this book.

12

Evaluate, Recover, Revise

In life we make the best mistakes we know how to make. Then,
with luck, we go out and make new ones.
                                    Joan Oliver Goldsmith

AN OLD FRIEND REMAINS CONFUSED

For a company that's more than two centuries old, Encyclopaedia
Britannica certainly is nimble. Maybe a little too nimble. Consider
its on-line strategy: The venerable publishing enterprise has flip-
flopped three times since 1994. As it handed out a second round of
pink slips, Britannica said it would return to charging customers
for access to its wealth of information on-line.

The company made its Web debut in 1994 with Britannica on-
line, a subscription service for colleges and universities. In 1995
Britannica extended the service to consumers, offering a subscription for $150 a year and eventually ratcheting down the price to
$50 a year. In October 1999, with only about 60,000 people signed
up, Britannica decided to offer itself at britannica.com free of charge,
relying on advertising for revenues. A couple of months later, it
repositioned itself as a portal and even advertised during the 2000

Super Bowl. But as the site tried to become a portal, it strayed from its branded competence with features like weather and stock information, and advertising revenues weren't strong enough to cover all the expenses.

Now Britannica officials say the company is going back to its roots, focusing on education and reference. It launched www.britannica school.com several months later.

Despite many years of success, Encyclopaedia Britannica is a company that demonstrates how not to handle a crisis; actually a series of crises. Clearly, their apparent unwillingness to employ a proactive crisis management plan has taken a bad situation and made it much worse. The situation appears quite desperate and the final outcome might prove to be actual survival.

Following the guidelines provided in this book, a company is able to effectively measure the outcome of their crisis management effort. In fact, it brings us to a point where three separate assessments are made: evaluation, recovery, and revision. The various elements of this assessment process are illustrated in Figure 12.1. It will guide our discussion for the remainder of this chapter.

IS IT OVER?

Strangely enough, one of the most difficult assessments to make is whether the crisis is over. Often, like a delayed fuse, just when you think the danger is over, there's another explosion. This is often the case. Take, for example, a case of sexual harassment, where witnesses come out of the woodwork when they see the initial complaint is successful. In a similar fashion, sometimes a crisis event has a domino effect that may take many weeks, or even months, to play out. The retirement of a key executive produces a whole series of possible moves by other executives, both within the organization and movement in and out.

Obviously, grading the success of a crisis plan before the impact of the event is over will likely provide inaccurate results. Although the duration of the impact will vary by crisis, as well as the related situation, there are a few guidelines that one might consider.

One indicator that the crisis is still viable is the fact that a great many questions are still being asked. These questions may be coming from customers, the general public, government agencies, and even competitors and employees. The fact that the media are still asking questions is probably the strongest indicator that the crisis still has some life. Hopefully, the information-monitoring process, especially the Internet, will gather these questions so that an intelligent judgment can be made.

Figure 12.1
The Crisis Assessment Process

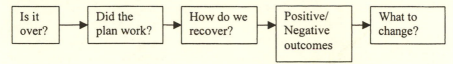

Somewhat related, a second indicator is the fact that the rumor mill is alive and well. As noted in an earlier chapter, rumors differ from directed questions in that they are not based on facts, but on inventors and subjective biases. Still, they can be very harmful, and can extend the life of a crisis for many weeks or months. There are a couple of things the crises manager might consider. First, attempt to collect these rumors and determine whether they have changed over time. Perhaps the latest set of rumors have little to do with the actual event in question. Second, assess where the rumors are coming from. There are some groups within an organization in which spreading rumors is normal operation, with very little credence. However, the rumors may be coming from a very important element within the organization, having significant implications.

A third factor, directly related to the first two, is whether employee morale is still affected. Even after all the lay-offs are finished, the employees who remain may continue to be very anxious and insecure for months afterward. Waiting for the hammer to drop may cause employees to seek other employment, sabotage work-related efforts, or go into clinical depression. Again, the information-gathering component of the crisis plan should include an employee-monitoring element that would address factors such as employee morale.

A final indicator that the crisis is still viable are the various measures of performance impacted by the crisis initially. Depending on the crisis, these measures might include share price, sales, profitability, returns, customer complaints, employee turnover, absenteeism, and so forth. These are fairly easily to monitor, and as long as they continue to be negative there is a strong indicator that the crisis is not over.

DID THE PLAN WORK?

In some respects, this may be an impossible question to answer. Hopefully, going through the effort of creating a crisis management plan has some important benefits. Otherwise, why do it? Still, these benefits are difficult to make tangible. Did the plan cause us to avoid crises altogether? Diminish the impact of those we did experience? In both instances, we hope the answer is yes.

It is suggested that conducting formal and informal research is necessary. Let's start with a survey of the relevant stakeholders. In the case of customers, we can survey them as to their level of satisfaction, how credible they feel the company is now that the crisis is over, and their level of trust toward the organization. We can also ask more macro questions, such as the general reputation of the organization. These same questions can be addressed to employees. Depending on the nature of the crises, we might also want to survey supplies, distributors, and legislators.

Less formal research can gather more qualitative information. Examples might include tracking the crisis-related stories appearing in the media. It would be encouraging if the stories tended to go from negative to positive, eventually disappearing. In addition to the media, it also would be informative to track the level of support from relevant organizations. For example, a labor union publicly stating that the organization was very professional and fair in contract negotiations would be a good sign. Or, the FDA announcing that you quickly and effectively made all the necessary changes would likewise bode well for the organization.

Another quite intangible measure of success is the general attitude of the people involved. Do you observe a higher level of confidence, less complaining, more positive discussions? Again, such observations are often hard to make, and may take a long time to appear, if ever. In cases where the crisis has a happy ending, the change may be obvious. A catastrophe causing loss of life may never produce such changes.

Part of this evaluation process should include a judgment of each of the plan's components. Did the crises management organization work? Did the control elements work? Did the communication strategy work? Did the classification matrix prove beneficial? Did the assessment of the internal and external environment prove accurate and beneficial? Were the correct stakeholders involved? Was the plan able to identify the actual causes of the crises? How did management and employees respond to the crisis plan? What part of the crises plan worked best? What part of the crises plan did not work well?

A final consideration, and by far the most explicit, is whether the crises plan achieved its stated objectives. Recall from Chapter 3 that there are two sets of crises-related objectives—proactive and reactive. That is, some of these objectives relate to activities before the crisis occurs, while others are directly related to the triggering event. The former might refer to training, developing a Web site, or identifying a spokesperson. The latter objectives are specific to the event, such as speed of reaction, communication sequencing, or restitution. Therefore, the crisis manager can easily compare actual performance with stated objectives. This should provide a good indicator of success.

HOW DO WE RECOVER?

Part of every crises plan should be a short-term and long-term recovery mechanism. Individuals in the middle of a crisis are rarely able to respond in an efficient and conscious manner. The recovery phase has several aspects, the most obvious of which is the attempt to recover what has been lost, which could involve tangible and intangible assets. This usually means managers have clearly identified in advance which items, processes, and personnel were absolutely necessary for implementing the recovery phase. Moreover, it is important to identify these elements in regards to internal operations as well as considerations outside the organization. If at all possible, the recovery mechanism should be pretested.

Short-term recovery plans might include the following concerns. Identifying minimal services and procedures to resume business should be an initial consideration. There might also be a need to move personnel, retrain, or find them new jobs. Moving part or all of your operation to another location might also be necessary.

Long-term recovery plans tend to deal with potential fixes that will prevent the crises from reoccurring. This might include considerations such as modernizing facilities, upgrading employee skill sets, installing a new security system, or putting in place a management transition plan. These long-term recovery initiatives need not necessarily be elaborate or expensive.

It All Depends on the Nature of the Crises

There is an interesting phenomenon that has a direct bearing on the recovery process. Often participants in the crisis event experience a type of cognitive bias. Such biases might include a decreased capacity to deal with complex problems, increased cognitive rigidity, inability to consider long-term issues, tendency to hang on to faulty solutions, and a faulty belief in invulnerability. All these biases have the potential to make recovery difficult, if not impossible. The crisis manager should be cognizant of these types of biases and prepare possible strategies to combat them. For example, providing employees with a written report about the crisis event and how it was effectively managed may prove helpful.

Positive or Negative Outcomes?

In Chapter 1 we indicated that a crisis event may actually have positive outcomes, and may even create heroes. Of course this is not always the case. And managers who look for a silver lining in every catastrophe are wasting a great deal of energy.

Despite the possibility that positive outcomes are possible, there is no systematic multidisciplinary perspective in how to analyze an event and cull out the benefits. For example, we can consider an explosion at a major production facility that caused three deaths, many injuries, destruction of technology as well as the existing social system. While appearing to be a totally negative outcome, it is conceivable that this same organization may experience a dramatic adjustment in employee morale that reestablishes self-integrity, motivation, and personal safety. But how do you measure these human characteristics? How long do they take to evolve and stabilize? The best you might be able to do is engage in observational research. In another case an organization's image is improved by the organization's effectiveness in managing the crisis event. Stock prices may even go up as a result of this management success.

The classic example of this outcome was how Johnson & Johnson handled the Tylenol case. Responding to the series of deaths that resulted from cyanide adulteration of Tylenol capsules, then CEO Jim Burke reasoned that forceful measures were needed to ensure public safety and restore trust in the company's top-selling product. With full page ads and television spots announcing its intentions, the company pulled 31 million capsules from store shelves and home medicine cabinets around the nation, redesigned the packaging, and within three months regained 95 percent of its precrisis market share. This feat was not accomplished without cost, but the cost of repurchasing a reputation that otherwise would have been severely tarnished would have been infinitely greater. From a business perspective, the result of the Tylenol crisis was that Johnson & Johnson demonstrated both its concern for its customers and its commitment to the corporation's ethical standards. Although this was a tragic episode, the company clearly was regarded even more highly after the event than before.

Because there is no standardized process in place to discern positive versus negative outcomes, it is recommended that research is necessary. To illustrate, let's look at the case of Snap-on, a $1.7 billion manufacturer of hand tools, primarily for mechanics, and industrial tools, such as automotive diagnostic equipment and hydraulic lifts. Snap-on lost a reported $50 million in sales during the first half of 1998 due primarily to snafus related to a new computer system. The new order-delivery system was intended to help dealer–customers order tools more quickly and easily, among other attributes. But once in place, the system didn't work properly and deliveries slowed significantly. In June of that year the company announced a restructuring, saying in a written statement that it would close five plants, cut 1,000 employees and take a $175 million restructuring charge; but the cost savings would be about $60 million annually. They also expect to close three Asian plants.

An initial step was for Snap-on to conduct research to determine whether customers are generally satisfied and leaving the company because of the problems of the moment, or if they are using the crisis situation as an excuse to act on dissatisfaction that had built up over other, more hidden issues. The company also decided to survey new customers, who have not yet built up loyalty to the firm but are critical to its future. It was also decided to do this research face-to-face, feeling that a telephone survey would be insulting to these professionals. They learned that doing this type of research was more difficult than expected. It was hard for customers to be truly objective, depending on how angry they were. Also, it is hard for the company to listen objectively and not want to answer.

In the end Snap-on learned that their customers were both loyal and forgiving. They appreciated the efforts to fix the computer glitch, and they particularly appreciated the willingness of Snap-on to ask them how they felt.

WHAT DID WE LEARN? WHAT DO WE CHANGE?

Someone wise once said, "You learn from every experience." Although this sounds like a truth, the fact remains that you don't learn from an experience unless you have a plan to do so. We all make the same mistakes over and over, so we obviously don't learn from our mistakes. A solid crisis plan should rectify this flaw and provide a mechanism for gathering the right information so that we might learn.

Learning refers to an individual's or organization's understanding of new ways of acting and acquisition of new skills as a result of an intervention. Do employees now understand how to acquire information from the company's Web site? Does top management now communicate more effectively with the media? Does corporate training now include sections relevant to the crisis event?

Once again, learning is a function of effective research. Perhaps an initial question to consider is the following: What successes in resolving the crisis event were a result of the crisis plan and what a result of dumb luck? The willingness of the crisis manager to take credit for dumb luck is appropriate, as long as he or she is willing to take credit for dumb bad luck. Luck is part of the crisis management equation. Deciphering which part of the outcome is strategy based and which part is luck based is an important exercise for continued learning. Business writer Robert Heller once said, "The first myth of management is that it exists. The second myth of management is that success equals skill."

Survey research (internal and external) focus groups, in-depth interviews, and Internet monitoring could provide the necessary information to make these decisions. Simply observing relevant stakeholders might also help you learn. Be forewarned that accessing whether learning has actually taken place is not easy. Many organizations would rather gloss over this phase because of the mistaken belief that an examination of the past will "only reopen old wounds." But almost the opposite has been found to be true. Following a crisis event, organizations with a crisis plan will be able to examine and compare, not assign blame, and make the necessary modifications in order to do better the next time. Still, people (including top management) are not always ready to learn. There is a great deal of anxiety with giving up something familiar and replacing it with something unfamiliar. The crisis manager must anticipate this and make every effort to reduce anxiety.

Epilogue

A concluding section that rounds out the design of a literary work.
Webster's Ninth New English Dictionary

POST–SEPTEMBER 11

Just as *Webster's* defines the epilogue, it tells us that a crisis is "an unstable or crucial time or state of affairs in which a decisive change is impending." As this book has proposed, the change can be great or small, positive or negative—but your company or organization has more of an impact on the degree of effect than previously allowed. If you have a plan in place, and the company has an enlightened view toward whether to even respond, disturbances can have not-so-critical impacts upon your operations. The origin of the word crisis is the Greek word *krisis*, which means choice. Even the ancient Greeks understood that crisis was something you can plan for.

SOUTHWEST AIRLINES

Geoffrey Colvin of *Fortune* magazine highlighted Southwest Airlines in his article "Smile! It's Recession Time," in the October 29,

2001 issue, by writing "after Sept. 11, I figured Southwest's profit streak, one of the most remarkable records in business—the company has made money every year for the past 28 years in a notoriously awful industry—was finally toast." He went on, however, to cite the multitude of reasons why his initial thoughts will probably prove to be false (at least at time of printing). He points out the major actions that differentiate the airline from its peers (who are currently facing crippling financial problems). Colvin cites the following salient facts in his piece: "Alone among major airlines, Southwest has not cut back operations. [Southwest] management actually believes it could show a profit for the year, and given that all other major carriers are going deeper into the hole every day (impairing their ability to invest, market, and hire for years to come, while Southwest stays in the black), Southwest is now worth more than all the other airlines in America combined."[1]

The following facts were issued by Southwest itself, and points to a very positive long-term situation:

1. Total operating losses incurred during the time operations were suspended (9/11/01–9/14/01) approximated $25 million.
2. Once operations were resumed, the company continued to incur operating losses through the end of the quarter of approximately $95 million due to depressed passenger traffic and revenues.
3. James F. Parker, vice chairman and CEO, stated the following in an October 18, 2001, press release by his company: "On September 14 we resumed operations and were operating our normal full schedule by September 18."
4. He also said, "As a result of the attacks . . . we have not placed into our schedule the eleven Boeing 737-700 aircraft originally scheduled for delivery from September 11–December 31, 2001. We are currently operating 100% of our fleet and, at this point, have no plans to ground any aircraft early."
5. "We are not contemplating any furloughs at this time," was another of Mr. Parker's positive statements.

All in all, revenue passengers carried by Southwest in 2001 totaled 49,450,492—up from 47,791,379 for the same nine-month period in the previous year. September 30, 2001, assets (excluding property and equipment) totaled $1,752,466,000—up from $831,536,000 for the same date in 2000. In general, things look good for Southwest Airlines.

"We Weren't Just Airborne Yesterday."

The first question that comes to any businessperson's mind is, How can they be doing that in the current environment? The short answer: Planning. Twenty-nine years ago, Rollin King and Herb Kelleher decided to start "a different kind of airline" and began with a simple premise: "If you get your passengers to their destinations when they want to get there, on time, at the lowest possible fares, and make darn sure they have a good time doing it, people will fly your airline."

Over the past twenty-eight years, Southwest has become the fifth largest major airline in America. They have won more than thirty Triple Crown awards for Best On-Time Record, Best Baggage Handling, and Fewest Customer Complaints, among other distinctions. But no one at Southwest could have foreseen the events of September 11, 2001—thirty years after their humble, three-aircraft beginnings. And that doesn't matter. Fortune-telling is not what you need to succeed at weathering a crisis. Planning is what crisis survival is all about.

Rather than reacting in a wave of communal response, and following their airline peers, Southwest did not lay off employees, they did not cut flights drastically, they did not retire aircraft. Because they were already "lean and mean" there was no need (or impetus to use the downturn as an excuse) to trim fat. Proper prior planning is more than just having a set reaction for every eventuality—it is keeping your organization in tip-top shape all the time. It is running lean every month. It is having clear lines of responsibility, and not changing your mind in a time of uncertainty. One of the founders, Herb Kelleher, had just turned over the roles of CEO to James Parker a few months before the terrorist attacks. Thus, even the succession planning process played a vital role in Southwest's survival.

The Future?

It could be argued that this has not been a crisis for the airline—or, as delineated earlier in the book, that Southwest management took the tack that sometimes no response is best. In fact, neither is true. The terrorist events of September 11 were just as devastating a crisis to Southwest Airlines as they were to Morgan Stanley, a company located in the north tower of the World Trade Center. The difference, however, is that Southwest had a proactive crisis plan in place. One that parallels the model portrayed in this book.

NOTE

1. The industry, on the other hand, expects the worst year in airline business history with losses totaling from $4 to $6 billion.

Bibliography

"Airfone Dramatically Drops Pricing as Special Outreach to its Airline Partners." *PRNewswire*, 27 September 2001.

Auerbach, Jon G., and William M. Bulkeley. "Web in Modern Age Is Arena for Activism, Terrorism, Even War." *The Wall Street Journal*, 10 February 2000, B4.

Augustine, Norman R. "Managing the Crisis You Tried to Prevent." *Harvard Business Review* (November–December 1995): 147.

Bailey, David. "Contest Fraud Probe Posed Ethical Dilemma for McDonald's." *Reuters Newswire*, 29 August 2001.

Barton, Laurence. *Crisis in Organizations II*. 2d ed. Cincinnati: South-Western, 2000.

Bottjen, Audrey. (Title not available). *Sales & Marketing Management*, September 2001, 48.

Bouwy, Sebastien. "France Adds Life to Coke." *The Denver Post*, 25 June 1999.

Bowler, Molly. "The Best PR Can't Fix Bad Business Decisions." *The Denver Business Journal*, 3–9 August 2001, 30A.

Burnett, John J. "A Strategic Approach to Managing Crises." *Public Relations Review*. JAI Press, 1998.

Byrnes, Nanette et al. "A Ruinous Day for Insurers." *Business Week*, 24 September 2001, 50.

Callahan , Patricia, and Amy Merrick. "Greeting-Card Firms Hasten to Serve Nation's New Mood." *The Wall Street Journal*, 4 October 2001, B4.

Campbell, Tricia. "Crisis Management at Coke." *Sales & Marketing Management* 14.

Caponigro, Jeffrey R. *The Crisis Counselor: A Step-by-Step Guide to Managing a Business Crisis.* New York: McGraw-Hill, 2000.

Carlson, Gustav. *Total Exposure: Controlling Your Company's Image in the Glare of the Business Media Explosion.* 1st ed. New York: AMACOM, 1999.

Carlzon, Jan. *Moments of Truth: New Strategies for Today's Customer-Driven Economy.* 2d ed. New York: Perennial Library, 1989.

"Cendant Comments on Financial Effect of Terrorist Attacks." *PRNewswire,* 28 September 2001.

Clendenning, Alan. "JetBlue Makes Cockpit Doors Bulletproof." *Rocky Mountain News,* 26 October 2001, 29A.

Cohn, Robin. *The PR Crisis Bible: How To Take Charge of the Media When All Hell Breaks Loose.* New York: St. Martin's Press, 2000.

Coombs, W. Timothy, and W. Timothy Coombs. *Ongoing Crisis Communication: Planning, Managing, and Responding.* Newbury Park, Calif.: Corwin Press, 1999.

"Delta SkyMiles® Program Offers Reduced Mileage Awards Through October 14." *PRNewswire,* 28 September 2001.

"'Department of Defense Labels Group Rations Packages to the Troops As Top Priority,' Says Ontro's V.P. Science and Engineering at Annual Meeting of Stockholders." *PRNewswire,* 1 October 2001.

"Disney Hopes to Help Children Cope." *Associated Press Newswire,* 27 September 2001.

Dolliver, Mark. "Energy, Or Lack Thereof." *ADWEEK,* 25 June 2001, 27.

Doughty, Ken, Ed. *Business Continuity Planning: Protecting Your Organization's Life.* Boca Raton, Fla.: CRC Press, 2000.

Echikson, William. "Have a Coke and a Smile—Please." *Business Week,* 30 August 1999, 214A.

Echikson, William, Stephen Baker, and Dean Foust. "Things Aren't Going Better With Coke." *Business Week.*

Ellison, Sarah. "Suddenly, Ads Once Considered Effective Are Now Tasteless after Terror Attacks." *The Wall Street Journal,* 19 September 2001, B12.

"Estee Lauder First-Quarter Earnings Rise." *Reuters Limited Newswire,* 25 October 2001.

Fink, Steven. *Crisis Management: Planning for the Inevitable.* IUniverse. com, 2000 (last accessed on January 8, 2001).

Gaines, Leslie-Ross. "CEO Driving Lessons." *Advertising Age,* 28 June 1999, 34.

Gillis, Tracy Knippenburg. *Emergency Exercise Handbook: Evaluate and Integrate Your Company's Plan.* Tulsa, Okla.: Penn Well, 1995.

Goldman, Debra. "Coke in Europe—When a Brand Means Too Much." *ADWEEK,* 23 August 1999, 16.

Gottesman, Alan. "Coping With Crisis." *ADWEEK,* 28 May 2001, 13.

Gullo, Karen. "8 Charged in Game Scam." *Rocky Mountain News,* 22 August 2001, 2A.

Harvard Business Review on Crisis Management. Boston: Harvard Business School Press, 2000.

Hennessey, Bernard. *Public Opinion*, 4th ed. Monterey, Calif.: Brooks/Cole, 1981.

Henry, Rene A. *You'd Better Have a Hose If You Want to Put Out the Fire: The Complete Guide to Crisis and Risk Communications*. 1st ed. Gollywobbler Productions, 2001.

Hiebert, Ray Eldon. "Public Relations as a Weapon of Modern Warfare." *Public Relations Review* (Summer 1991): 107.

Hilsenrath, Jon E. "Terror's Toll on the Economy." *The Wall Street Journal*, 9 October 2001, B1.

Hirschman, Albert O. "Exit, Voice and Loyalty: Further Reflections and a Survey of Recent Contributions." *Social Science Information* 13 (1) (1973):9.

Jackson, Janice E., and William T. Schantz. "Crisis Management Lessons: When Push Shoved Nike." *Business Horizons* (January–February 1993): 27.

Janis, Irving Lester. *Crucial Decisions: Leadership in Policymaking and Crisis Management*. New York: Free Press, 1989.

Jones, Del. "Terrorism Takes Toll on Many Industries." *USA Today*, 14 September 2001, B1.

Kamins, Michael A., Valerie S. Folkes, and Lars Perner. "Consumer Responses to Rumors: Good News, Bad News." *Journal of Consumer Psychology* (1997).

Kauffman, James. "NASA in Crisis: The Space Agency's Public Relations Efforts Regarding the Hubble Space Telescope." *Public Relations Review* (1997): 1.

Kilburn, David. "Letter from Asia: Coping With Crisis." *ADWEEK*, 9 February 1998, 22.

Kolesar, Oeter. "Vision, Values, Milestones: Paul O'Neill Starts Total Quality at ALCOA." *California Management Review* (Spring 1993): 162.

Levitt, Alan M. *Disaster Planning and Recovery: A Guide for Facility Professionals*. New York: John Wiley & Sons, 1997.

Lukaszewski, James E., and James M. Alexander. *Corporate Activism on the Internet: Rogue Activist Web Sites*. Lukaszewski Group, 1999.

Lukaszewski, James E., and Mary Ann N. Cotton. *First Response: Critical First Response Steps/A Management Model for Effective Response to Crisis*.Lukaszewski Group, 1996.

MacArthur, Kate. "McSwindle: McDonald's Alliance with Simon Ends after FBI Uncovers $13 Million Prize Theft." *Advertising Age*, 27 August 2001, 1.

Machalaba, Daniel, and Carrick Mollenkamp. "Companies Struggle to Cope with Chaos, Breakdowns and Trauma." *The Wall Street Journal*, 13 September 2001, B1.

"Make a Flag, Make a Difference; Toys 'R' Us Sponsors Flag Drawing Fundraiser for Kids." *PRNewswire*, 27 September 2001.

Marconi, Joe. *Crisis Marketing: When Bad Things Happen to Good Companies*. 2d ed. New York: McGraw-Hill, 1997.

McGrath, Joan, and Myrna Pedersen. "Don't Wait for Disaster; Have Crisis Plan Ready." *Marketing News*, 2 December 1996, 6.

Meyers, Gerald C., and Susan Meyers. *Dealers, Healers, Brutes and Saviors: Eight Winning Styles for Solving Giant Business Crises.* 1st ed. New York: John Wiley & Sons, 2000.

Miles, Stephanie. "Free E-mail Web Sites Can Be a Backup in Emergencies." *The Wall Street Journal*, 27 September 2001, B10.

Mitroff, Ian I., ed. *Managing Crises before They Happen: What Every Executive Needs to Know about Crisis Management.* 1st ed. New York: AMACOM, 2000.

Mitroff, Ian I., ed. *The Essential Guide to Managing Corporate Crises: A Step-by-Step Handbook for Surviving Major Catastrophes.* Book & Disk ed. New York: Oxford University Press, 1996.

Murphy, Victoria. "Quicksand." *Forbes*, 9 July 2001, 50–51.

Myers, Kenneth N. *Manager's Guide to Contingency Planning for Disasters: Protecting Vital Facilities and Critical Operations.* 2d ed. New York: John Wiley & Sons, 1999.

Nudell, Mayer, and Norman Antokol. *The Handbook for Effective Emergency and Crisis Management.* Reprint ed. Mayer Nudell, 1999.

Ogrizek, Michel, Jen-Michel Guillery, and Helen Kimball-Brooke. *Communicating in Crisis.* Hawthorne, N.Y.: Aldine de Gruyter, 1999.

Orenstein, Susan. "'Our Focus Had to Be on People.'" *Business 2.0* (November 2001): 30–31.

Pauchant, Thierry C., and Ian I. Mitroff. *Transforming the Crisis-Prone Organization: Preventing Individual, Organizational, and Environmental Tragedies.* San Francisco: Jossey-Bass, 1992.

Pierce, Ellise. "A Crushing Wave of Wood." *Newsweek*, 29 November 1999, 44.

Pinsdorf, Marion K. *Communicating When Your Company Is Under Siege: Surviving Public Crisis.* 3d ed. New York: Fordham University Press, 1999.

Ray, Sally J. *Strategic Communication in Crisis Management.* Westport, Conn.: Quorum Books, 1999.

"Roper Reports: The Mood of the Nation." *RoperASW/NOP World*, 24 September 2001.

Rose, Matthew. "In Its Rush, *People* Neglects Advertisers." *The Wall Street Journal*, 19 September 2001, B12.

Schmidt, Kathleen V. "Coke's Crisis." *Marketing News*, 27 September 1999, 1.

Sellers, Patricia. "Coke's CEO Doug Daft Has to Clean Up: The Big Spill." *Fortune*, 6 March 2000, 58.

Sells, Bill. "What Asbestos Taught Me About Managing Risk." *Harvard Business Review* (March–April 1994): 76.

Silva, Michael, ed. *Overdrive: Managing in Crisis-Filled Times (New Directions in Business).* 2d ed. New York: John Wiley & Sons, 1995.

Slater, Jeremy, and Laurel Wentz. "Coke Taps Publicist to Stanch Crisis." *Advertising Age*, 21 June 1999, 50.

Smith, Amie. "Coke's European Resurgence." *PROMO* (December 1999): 91.

Solomon, Deborah, and Shawn Young. "Restoring Phone, Data Services Will Take Months." *The Wall Street Journal*, 14 September 2001, B3.

Southwest Airlines Web site, October 24, 2001.

Starbucks Coffee Company Web Site. Press release, "Statement Re: Bottled Water Incident During the September 11, 2001 Tragedy." 25 September 2001.

Strauss, Gary. "Informant Key to Unlocking Scam Behind Golden Arches." *USA Today*, 24 August 2001, B1.

Tully, Shawn. "From Bad to Worse." *Fortune*, 15 October 2001, 118–128.

"UPDATE: McDonald's Continuing Response to National Tragedy." *PRNewswire*, 28 September 2001.

Weber, Thomas E. "After Terror Attacks, Companies Rethink Role of Face-to-Face." *The Wall Street Journal*, 24 September 2001, B1.

Wells, Melanie. "Anticlimax: Sam Shahid's Racy Ads." *Forbes*, 20 March 2000, 58.

Winter, Matthias, and Ulrich Steger. *Managing Outside Pressure: Strategies for Preventing Corporate Disasters*. 2d ed. New York: John Wiley & Sons, 1998.

Woodyard, Chris. "Airlines' Voluntary Steps Fall Short With Fliers." *USA Today*, 9 January 2001, 14B.

Zimmerman, Eileen. "Catch the Bug." *Sales and Marketing Management* (February 2001): 79.

Index

ABOUT THE AUTHOR

John Burnett is professor of marketing, University of Denver, and Chairperson of Denver University's marketing department. Author of more than thirteen earlier books, including four widely used textbooks, he has published in all the major academic journals of his field. Dr. Burnett concentrates his research on marketing communication strategy, segmentation, and services marketing, and has consulted with numerous companies, such as Johnson & Johnson, Qwest, AT&T, Lucent, and First Data.

DATE DUE
